What do you
think I could
do to help you

LUCIFER AND THE SCHOOLTEACHER

The Trauma and Healing of Racism in American Education

DR. DEBRA HOBBS

BALBOA.PRESS
A DIVISION OF HAY HOUSE

Balboa Press books may be ordered through booksellers or by contacting:

Balboa Press
A Division of Hay House
1663 Liberty Drive
Bloomington, IN 47403
www.balboapress.com
844-682-1282

Because of the dynamic nature of the Internet, any web addresses or links contained in this book may have changed since publication and may no longer be valid. The views expressed in this work are solely those of the author and do not necessarily reflect the views of the publisher, and the publisher hereby disclaims any responsibility for them.

The author of this book does not dispense medical advice or prescribe the use of any technique as a form of treatment for physical, emotional, or medical problems without the advice of a physician, either directly or indirectly. The intent of the author is only to offer information of a general nature to help you in your quest for emotional and spiritual well-being. In the event you use any of the information in this book for yourself, which is your constitutional right, the author and the publisher assume no responsibility for your actions.

Any people depicted in stock imagery provided by Getty Images are models, and such images are being used for illustrative purposes only.
Certain stock imagery © Getty Images.

Author photo by Kia Caldwell Photography

Scripture quotations are taken from the Holy Bible, New Living Translation, copyright © 1996, 2004, 2015 by Tyndale House Foundation. Used by permission of Tyndale House Publishers, Inc., Carol Stream, Illinois 60188. All rights reserved.

Scripture quotations marked KJV are from the Holy Bible, King James Version (Authorized Version). First published in 1611. Quoted from the KJV Classic Reference Bible, Copyright © 1983 by The Zondervan Corporation

Print information available on the last page.

ISBN: 978-1-9822-6578-6 (sc)
ISBN: 978-1-9822-6580-9 (hc)
ISBN: 978-1-9822-6579-3 (e)

Library of Congress Control Number: 2021905744

Balboa Press rev. date: 03/18/2021

Dedicated to

Edna & Marvin and Martha & Ransome
for setting the earthly foundation

Arianna and Jocie
for bringing heaven to my earthly existence

Contents

But I say unto you, Love your enemies, bless them that curse you, do good to them that hate you, and pray for them which despitefully use you, and persecute you.
—Matthew 5:44 (KJV)

Preface

HEAVEN'S GATE IS never closed to us. While we are on earth in this dimension, achieving paradise is ever present and possible, if we *elect* it. Satan has a permanent contract with no possibility for free agency; heaven's gate is closed to this entity for an eternity. Lucifer, however, having declared war on the divine Creator while still in heaven, has the possibility of hope—hope to choose virtue; hope to choose justice and honesty; hope to always choose love. Hatred can be eradicated, if we choose to do it. Writing about my trauma and sharing it enables Lucifer moments to subside; understanding my story may open your story, and together, we can germinate healing.

Introduction

COVID-19 PROVIDED AN everlasting snow day for students and teachers. At least, it did for me, initially. I started getting caught up on some much-needed rest, and a quiet opportunity to grade the endless stacks of papers (an English teacher's constant dilemma) presented itself. I felt peaceful. *Finally,* I thought, *I have some time to be still; I have some time to practice mindfulness.* However, the recurrent email notifications regarding our return and yet another extended deadline for our return bewildered my mind and disorganized my lesson plans. The lack of human contact with my students, colleagues, family, and friends presented an alarming void. How was I going to say goodbye to my seniors? I always plan a special series of closure classes for my kids, as we teachers affectionately call our students. How was I going to return Sydney's self-portrait? How would my nonfiction classes do their film documentary? What new entries would Ethan add to his "Plague" journal? Did I have enough toilet paper? Yes, I was one of those folks who became panic-stricken about not having enough milk, eggs, bread, and other household essentials. How was my daughter going to survive her senior year of college life in Washington, DC? She, like so many other senior-year students around the globe, had worked so rigorously and strategically toward the 2020 graduation year. So many critical rites of passage were lost in the quiet mutiny of the world pandemic. Why now? My mind began to crave answers for a seemingly irrational viral outbreak. So I began to spend my more than ample spare moments reading Eckhart Tolle's *A New Earth*; Gary Zukav's *Seat of the Soul*; Michael Singer's *The Untethered Soul: The Journey Beyond Yourself*; *The Law of Attraction* by Grace Bell; *Talking to Heaven* by James Van Praagh; Wayne Dyer's *Your Erroneous Zones*; Diane Stein's *Psychic Healing*; *Afterlife* by Barry Eaton; *Journey of Souls* by Dr. Michael Newton; *The Mastery of Love* by Don Miguel Ruiz; the King James Version of the Bible; and a host of many other books—too many to mention. Well, I figured that I should either prepare for the end of the world or at the bare minimum reflect on how to become a more adaptable person. If this proved to be an actual apocalypse, then I wanted to be able to handle heaven or hell with some good strategic plans, or at least be able to use my words for a decent line of defense should I need one. If this moment was not an apocalyptic one, then I needed to handle my earthly existence more gracefully.

Slowly, I began to settle into the media's term of "the new normal." I created new lesson plans and reworked old lesson plans to suit the environment of full-scale remote learning. Email became the primary means for my students and me to connect on more personal and individual levels. Zoom meetings were supposed to bridge the separation of our humanity. Although students and teachers were really suffering from our new disconnection, we used our profession of hope to rally our troops. I commenced living in the present and thought quite infrequently about the past and the future. I missed my kids, but I discovered some fascinating ways of thinking and being. Knowing that all of my children were safe, my leisurely "think" time became "me" time, an unfamiliar privilege for a single mom with an honorable and demanding career. Watching Governor Andrew Cuomo's composure and listening to his eloquent articulation of strategy for New York State, combined with his designs to quell the resurgence of COVID-19 and scaffold the reopening of his constituency, bestowed a sense of calm in me. A most peculiar reaction, I know. Being a native Pennsylvanian, I appreciate and applaud Governor Wolf's guidance; however, Governor Cuomo had a regular and active presence on television in which he provided the incremental steps being taken to address the fears and concerns consuming my mind. He never camouflaged the realities we faced, and he never retreated from his resolve to protect all citizens. I watched and listened to him every day! Despite the many unknown variables surrounding the spreading virus, I was learning to cope fairly well; I just needed a little more laughter in my world.

On May 25, 2020, "me" time turned into a fight for my life! I say this because watching a YouTube video of Mr. George Floyd's assassination (yes, I mean it—assassination, not murder) over and over and over and over again brought me to the abyss of hatred.

CHAPTER 1

Lucifer a.k.a. Hatred

AFTER SUFFERING EMOTIONAL, psychological, and spiritual trauma watching George Floyd's tragic demise, I was forced into confronting my own demons—specifically, hatred. I waited desperately for some of my closest friends, who are White, to reach out to me via a phone call, not a text, not an email, and not a visit because of COVID-19. Combine this with social media hate speech and uninformed yet presumptive comments in professional Zoom meetings and years of systemic racism, and I began to hate White people.

Yes, I know—horrible, but so true. I was still seething from watching Ava DuVernay's 2019 four-part series *When They See Us,* a true account of five African American men who were wrongfully convicted and sent to prison as teenagers for raping a White woman jogging in Central Park in 1989. Years of internal pain and suffering unlocked the door to rage. My unbridled rage opened the shutters and windows and invited hatred to rest quietly in my heart for a spell. Even in the midst of these very moments, I knew that my emotional mindset was unhealthy, counterproductive, and immoral.

However, I allowed myself to fully absorb the noise of my mind. "The voice in the head tells a story that the body believes in and reacts to. Those reactions are the emotions. The emotions, in turn, feed energy back to the thoughts that created the emotion in the first place. This is the vicious circle between unexamined thoughts and emotions, giving rise to emotional thinking and emotional story-making."[1]

My spell of hatred induced frequent migraine headaches, bouts of yelling, vomiting, and overall unhealthiness. The research-proven connection between "negative emotional states and physical disease" lacks stamina in "mainstream medicine."[2] However, the impact of a negative mindset on family and friends can directly trigger a chain reaction and indirectly hoist a chain of negative energy upon the universe. "There is a generic term for all negative emotions: unhappiness."[3]

I was internally and externally unhappy. And I knew why. Although my upbringing, like that of many folks, hadn't affirmed total bliss, I had two loving parents who had raised me to "love thy neighbor as thyself." Unfortunately, self-love is an acquired, long-suffering achievement. I suspect that this may be the case for most if not all of us.

Where do I go from here? I wondered. How could I move forward knowing that my mind and heart harbored such deep-seated resentment, anger, and disillusionment?

While running some "essential" errands, I discovered a tinge of humor in my situation as I wore my COVID-19 mask. Despite the painful realities unfolding in front of me every day, despite the fact that members of my community were branded, hunted, killed, and dehumanized, my mask was supposed to protect others. How terribly paradoxical! How terribly peculiar! How terribly real!

I slowly began to realize that I now embodied the very hatred that I despised, and I slowly began to understand hatred from an intimate place. Suddenly, amid my sobering thoughts, I developed a comprehension of racism. If I allowed my bruised psyche to continue on its journey, my behavior would begin to match and extend my thoughts. The possibility that I might, in fact, begin to use my hatred for White people as a means to seek revenge, punishment, and ultimately payback ricocheted me back to a place of pain. However, this time the noise of my mind resounded with shame.

I began to unpack my shame, my hatred, and yes, my brief and fleeting racist thoughts. Organized by African American students, a committed and unswerving adult at my school, and my place of employment, a local Black Lives Matter protest joined the countless other Black Lives Matter protests around the globe. Surprised and amazed, I saw many of my White friends and colleagues at the protest, *and* they brought along their children to an event benefiting my African American community, all in the middle of a worldwide pandemic. Essentially, they were willing to risk contracting a potentially deadly virus for me! At least, my ego placed me in the delicate chambers of their hearts.

After the protest concluded, I chose to secure a still moment with my daughter to talk openly and honestly about George Floyd, and we cried. Because of our deep friendship of respect and continuously open lines of communication, tears and hugs heaved me into sobering self-criticism. Even though my daughter has refused to watch Alex Huxley's *Roots*, Ava DuVernay's *When They See Us*, and other influential cultural works, she has lived the life of an African American female and intimately feels and understands the pain and the hatred.

Her refusal to watch the pain in full color on-screen is actually a testament to her innocence. On many occasions, she has warned me that watching her people suffer at the hands of White people would make her hate them. I have always been afraid that her limited exposure to painful truths captured in films and texts might blind her to a full understanding of systemic racism or might somehow instill an intolerable ignorance of our people. But we have shed too many tears during her twenty-two years of existence over racist school leaders, racist school decisions, racist schoolteachers, racist school friends, racist school curricula, and so on.

She gets it, and so do I. My daughter handles "it" better than I do. I told her that many of my White friends and colleagues had marched in protest alongside me. She said, "Of course, a lot of White teachers were there, Mom, because they care too." My body caved in. I tearfully dropped to the ground simply because I realized I had been blessed with a young woman who loved humanity with all of its textures, colors, genders, religions, appearances, political affiliations, strengths, and weaknesses.

Parents would love to accept complete credit for their child's upbringing. But I know better. Most of the time, my daughter allows her spiritual side to speak and act; she seems to me to be in complete alignment with her divine Creator. Most of the spiritual teachers I have mentioned and will continue to mention boldly assert that we are two in one: spiritual self and earthly self.

Sadly, I learned that Lucifer had decided to take up a brief residence in my heart and compromise my humanity. Serious reflection taught me that when I plunged into the abyss of hating White people, I had decided to dance with Lucifer.

It was time to examine my thoughts and rewrite this emotional narrative. It was time to heal my personal pain and begin the journey toward understanding others more profoundly. It was time to wrestle with racist ideology. It was time to love racists who, in reality, are no different than you or me. I was having what I would like to call an ecclesiastical moment!

Despite the war between various races, ethnicities, religions, genders, socioeconomic statuses, colors, and creeds, isn't it *a time to love* (Ecclesiastes 3:8 KJV)? Aren't we tired of fighting? Aren't we exhausted from plucking, killing, weeping, and mourning? Can we stop stoning, losing, shredding, hating, and casting away?

Despite the outward appearance of our painful realities, this is the time for rebuilding, planting, healing, laughing, and dancing. We should be gathering, embracing, getting, keeping, sewing, and speaking.

I, like so many peaceful protestors around the globe, have chosen to speak. Unfortunately, all of us are not marching together peacefully. But I understand. I understand that we have faced individual and communal traumas that blind our true spiritual selves and distort our soul's missions. Sometimes each and every one of us allows destructive noise to develop within our head and heart. We need to face the fact that as members of humanity, we share a collective understanding of trauma.

Somewhere on trauma's continuum, we all sit, stand, and breathe. As we sit, stand, and breathe in our personal traumas, we can choose to invite a vile guest into our home, or we can choose to ask the vile guest to leave. Hatred doesn't choose us—we elect hatred.

CHAPTER 2

Trauma, Part One

LUCIFER IS A free agent. As a free agent he doesn't have a contract per se. He may solicit offers from any other prospective teams. Starting at 7:57 p.m. on the evening of March 25, 2020, teams began to negotiate deals with Lucifer. With no early termination option in sight, Lucifer signed the contract with most of us after eight minutes and forty-six seconds. My recording-time deal with Lucifer is not being paraded as a point of pride. In fact, my contractual agreement is a result of sustained trauma.

I was born an African American female, "de mule of de world"[4] and the one "everybody in the world was in a position to give orders [to],"[5] according to Zora Neale Hurston and Toni Morrison, respectively. I knew my placement the moment I emerged into Piaget's world of "equilibration"—I didn't really matter.

Jean Piaget conceived a model describing the process humans undergo as they begin to make sense of their world. His system of gathering and organizing information formed a theory of cognitive development analogous to the changes found in the mollusk. According to Piaget, as young people develop in accordance with their genetic potential, they change their behavior to adapt to their environment.

One of the factors influencing development is *equilibration*.[6] As the word implies, a young person is searching for balance. If a young person encounters a certain situation or event and applies a certain way of thinking or motor pattern of development to the event and achieves a satisfying result, then equilibrium exists. But if the scheme does not produce a satisfying result, disequilibrium exists. The person becomes uncomfortable. Well, if I use Piaget's theory as a gauge, I have been in a state of disequilibrium for most of my life.

I speculate that most other members of my community have been in this exact state of mind as well. We are just confused, and simply put, we are moving into a state of rage.

My first childhood crush centered on a young White boy who looked like Brad Pitt and acted like young Justin Bieber. He was smart, sassy, and intoxicating. I will call him Xavier. Xavier seemed to really like me; we would often exchange love notes and walk to the cafeteria together, and everybody, including most of his guy friends, told me that Xavier adored me. Sometimes we would slip away during a shared class and go make out in the dark abandoned hallways next to the school gymnasium. We even shared our lunches, if he decided to abandon his guy friends and sit with me during our lunch periods. He would give me his apple, and I would surrender my Del Monte mixed fruit salad packed in sweet syrup. On school class trips, Xavier would always walk slightly ahead of me, then secretively reach his hand back for me to grab his hand. We would secretly hold hands until someone noticed and yelled, "Look at the two lovebirds over there," and he would then quickly drop my hand. Yes, this was my bliss at twelve to seventeen years of age. Interracial dating was still taboo in the 1970s and '80s, yet we were "quite the couple," as all our classmates stated.

When senior year of high school arrived, my excitement for the prom proved overwhelming. I knew that my maternal grandmother would make my gown, and my mom would press and curl my hair, and I would be so well loved and admired because my relationship had withstood the test of time. Xavier and I were in love, or at least, so I thought. As time moved closer to the actual date of the prom and my grandmother finally finished my beautiful white silk organza dress, I wondered when Xavier was going to officially ask me to go with him to the prom. When I finally summoned enough courage to ask him about our prom plans, he quietly said, "Oh, Deb, I asked someone else to go with me." Staring blankly back at him, I said, "Oh." Needless to say, my heart, shattered and broken, still remembers the pain of this surprise rejection! Of course, there was drama surrounding the details of this horrible moment, but in my total confusion, I sought solace in hatred. No, I didn't hate Xavier; I thought Xavier hated me because I was Black! It just didn't make sense that we were not going to the prom together. What did make sense to me was the fact that he had asked a White girl named Jackie. She had soft brown hair with blonde highlights and blue eyes. Even as I type this story into public existence, gentle tears still fall down my face. This became the first story among a lifetime of Lucifer stories. Some of the stories show a movement toward self-hatred.

Religion, legend, and folklore support the story that Lucifer, also known as the morning star, became so impressed with his own beauty, intelligence, power, and position that he began to desire for himself the honor and glory that belonged to God. As punishment, God tossed this angel out of heaven forever, and Lucifer became the fallen angel known as Satan. **Therefore, Lucifer moments occur when the ego seeks complete fulfillment.** These can be moments of penetrating hatred or rage, sorrow, depression, disillusionment, shame, doubt, worry, and disappointment. I hypothesize that hatred of any kind results from some type of trauma and arises out of the emotional life formed in the limbic system of the brain. When this system is triggered, painful memories awaken, causing a person to relive the trauma, and the consequences of reliving sustained trauma will manifest extremely undesirable thoughts and behaviors. Hell on earth is possible. Hypothetically speaking, racists have experienced trauma, and their worries, fears, angers, and hurts get activated by their strong desire for ego fulfillment. I know because it happened to me.

CHAPTER 3

Help Me Heal, or Keep It Movin'

HOW WOULD YOU answer these questions?

- **What would you do if someone called you a "nigger"?**

It happened in third grade, right before my parents transferred me to another school. My parents had always instilled the idea that education would set me free. My mind was a sanctuary and a harbor of choice, and I should cherish it and protect it. My mom always did her research before she signed any contractual agreements. She weighed options; she configured transportation; she organized a budget; she contemplated cultural concerns. My parents never presented a deficit model for me; they didn't care if I might be the only Black child in a school or class. In fact, I didn't even know that I was Black until I was around eight years old and in the third grade of a very prestigious Catholic school managed by an order of Franciscan nuns. I learned much later in life that Grace Kelly had attended the school as well. My memory furnishes the story to the best of its ability. I was enjoying my free time by climbing the trees on campus. I have always loved caterpillars; I used to stroke their hairy, soft bodies and grant them access to my arms, legs, and face. I would find them on trees and sometimes the ground, and I would gather as many of them as I could, gently carrying them to my special spot in the grass near a statue of a patron saint—I can't remember the saint. After placing some of the caterpillars on my arms, legs, and face, I would fall back into the grass. I would close my eyes while I sensed their slow furry movements on my body. This served as my bliss in third grade. I didn't need a friend, and I didn't need to play duck-duck-goose; I just needed a moment of peace with my soon-to-be butterflies. I always knew that my furry friends would grow into butterflies with brightly colored wings. I hoped to watch the process and, in some way, assist their journey. I didn't know any of the detailed biology, but I thought if I held them enough and allowed enough room on my skin, I would be granted an opportunity to see them change.

Well, one day I had just finished opening a huge nest of caterpillars, and I was getting ready to place some of them in my lunch box with cheese curls for their nourishment. Two of my White classmates (I will call them Mary and Kate) approached and said in a soft voice, "Hey, nigger." Just like that—no warning, no preparation, no other taunting words as a precedent. To my recollection, I really didn't know what they had said initially. In fact, I had never heard that word in my life. I blankly stared at them, and then they repeated it more loudly: "Hey, nigger." I don't know what happened to me or what I must have been thinking, but I started laughing and saying the word "nigger" myself. I repeated it over and over, much to their delight. Mary and Kate doubled over in laughter and said, "Why are you saying that word? That's what you are." I stopped laughing. They did too. Then they just walked away, and I stood there with my hands filled with soft, furry, and now slipping caterpillars.

I told my mom the story and asked her if I was a "nigger." She told me that she had been called the same word on her job, and she then proceeded to tell me the response she had publicly given to her coworker. My mom said, "We are all niggers." Essentially, my mom called every human being the N-word. Later, in the evening after dinner, I found out that I was Black. My mom took me to the mirror and showed me the differences between my skin, hair, nose, and lips and White people's features. She informed me that White people used this racial slur to dehumanize us. I don't think I fully understood any of the lessons that day. I just remember finally opening my school lunch box to discover that my caterpillars were dead.

- **What would you say or do if a teacher nun physically shook you, placed you in a closet, and said, "You are evil and naughty"?**

At the same prestigious Catholic school, I saw my first Black nun. She was one of my teachers. I remember just looking at her, wondering how a Black woman had become a nun. Sister Betty was rotund. She walked heavily, moved hurriedly, and spoke viciously. But I loved Sister Betty because she looked like me. I would always try to sit next to her during story time so that I could secretively clasp her hand. I just wanted to feel what it would be like to hold a teacher's hand that looked like my hand. My White nun teachers always held my hands; the warmth from their smiles, words of encouragement, and patient guidance made me feel safe and loved. But the hands of the other sisters didn't look like mine. I wanted to hold Sister Betty's hands the most. But there was one problem with Sister Betty: she smelled bad. She reeked, quite frankly, of body odor. It upset me when my classmates made fun of her by calling her Sister Stinky or Sister B, the latter of which she thought was a nickname like B for Betty. It was Sister B for body odor without the O.

My friends and I decided that it would be best if someone told her that she stank. Guess who got nominated and eagerly accepted? Yes, me. That's right, caterpillar Debra was ready to assist Sister Betty's journey now. I was ready to release my Black sister teacher from her odorous reputation. While Sister Betty was walking to the back of the open classroom, I asked to speak with her privately. "Yes, dear one," she responded. I grabbed one of her hands and motioned for her to stoop down because I had to tell her something in her ear. I said, "Sister Betty, you stink." Just like that—no warning, no preparation, no other advisory words as a precedent. Well, Sister Betty dropped my hand, grabbed both of my shoulders, shook me several times, and said, "You are an evil and naughty child." Then she grabbed me by one shoulder, walked me briskly and heavily to the arts and crafts supply closet, pushed me into the darkened closet, closed the door, and locked it. After I sat for seemingly two to three hours on the cold floor, huddled up and afraid to move because of the ghosts who lived in the closet, Sister Betty opened the door to freedom. I slowly walked out with my head down, quite ashamed of myself, and Sister Betty said, "Now go back to your desk and finish your work."

My friends rushed over to me and asked what had happened. I just put my head down on the desk and began to cry as silently as I could. I didn't share this story with my parents until after I had graduated high school. My Black teacher had made me hate her and myself. Academically speaking, Sister Betty was the first rung of my educational ladder toward self-understanding. She destabilized my ascent.

- **How do you prevent a teacher nun's inappropriate behavior?**

I auditioned for and won the role of Mary in our school play, *The Nativity*. I couldn't wait to go home and tell my parents and grandparents the good news. My mommom was so excited that she told me that she was going to make a special swaddling cloth for my baby Jesus. My mom loved to shop at thrift stores for good buys. We call this shopping "vintage" today. My mom actually found an African American porcelain baby at a thrift store. We were so pleasantly surprised. My mom and my mommom and I were a team, and quite often, they would bring me along on shopping sprees for groceries, clothes, shoes, and pantyhose a.k.a. stockings. Some of my favorite moments were having lunch together in the café market near the big brown bronze boar in the Strawbridge & Clothier store in Center City, Philadelphia. We would sit there for hours, just eating, talking, and laughing after a shopping spree.

So when my mom brought home this latest treasure, we banned together, making a "fuss," as my mommom would say, over the preparations for my role in the annual Christmas play. There was one problem. Another classmate, Julia, who also had auditioned for the part of Mary, just cried every single day about not getting the part and pressured Sister Margaret to let her play Mary for at least one of the performances. She got her wish.

During rehearsals, I proudly coddled my Black baby Jesus wrapped in a special swaddling cloth that my mommom had sewn together. My mommom was a gifted seamstress; she made every winter coat that I wore until I was eighteen years old. She made every prom dress and every formal dress that I needed until I was twenty-three years old. If the arthritis in her hands had not prevented her from continuing to sew for me, she also would have sewn my wedding gown because she had made my mother's wedding gown and the wedding gowns of many young women from our church. I loved my mom and mommom so much; they were my rocks of Gibraltar.

Well, Sister Margaret asked if Julia could borrow my baby Jesus for her performance; I agreed with the understanding that I would get him back in time for my performances. Sister Margaret, a White nun, always seemed to love the Black and brown children. I remember her telling the class that Jesus probably looked like me. I was shocked. *Huh?* I thought. But if Sister Margaret said Jesus looked like me, I had no problems with her lessons. In fact, I loved the idea; it gave me a little pep in my step. I felt regal, refined, and special. When Sister Margaret spoke to me, she always got really close to my face and stared deeply into my eyes and stroked my back a lot. I didn't think anything about her behavior was erratic at the time, until my mom got involved. I would come home and share my day with all of the adults in my home; it was our daily routine to share. As my family listened attentively to my experiences with Sister Margaret, they must have been cataloging every detail.

When Julia completed her performance, my baby Jesus allegedly disappeared, and I couldn't use my Black baby Jesus wrapped in my mommom's specially sewn swaddling cloth for my performances. The school community collected a group of White dolls from which I could choose. I chose a White-skinned, yellow-haired rag doll to use as my new baby Jesus. My team mobilized. My mother asked Sister Margaret about my Black baby Jesus, and my mommom went to the school looking for my Black baby Jesus, but it wasn't found.

My Black baby Jesus came home to me three years later, after I had transferred out of the school. Sister Margaret came to my home and rang the bell, and I opened the door. I couldn't believe my eyes. Sister Margaret was standing in front of me with those piercing eyes, holding my Black baby Jesus wrapped in my mommom's specially sewn swaddling cloth. My parents and grandparents were at work. I had only a babysitter with me, and she was very old, or at least that is my childhood memory. Sister Margaret told me that my "doll" had been found and she just wanted to return it to me. Three years later? She gave me the doll, as she called it, and hugged me, kissed me on the forehead, and patted me on the back several times. I told her, "Thank you." Then she left, and I closed the door.

Mrs. Winston, my babysitter, didn't even know I had answered the door. Mrs. Winston was fired, and my mom warned me to never speak with Sister Margaret again. This was the second rung of my educational ladder toward self-understanding. My White sister teacher who had made me feel royal, special, and beloved potentially had immoral intentions.

- **What would you do if someone called you a "nigger" again?**

I was older now and attending a Quaker school. The mission of the school and the nonviolent approach to conflict appealed to my mother. My dad felt that I should attend a public school, but my mother paid for every educational journey I took. If my mom was paying the tuition, then my dad didn't have a problem with my attending private schools. So now I was at a school in which I referred to my White male teachers as "Master" and my White female teachers as "Teacher." Isn't hindsight the best foresight?

In fifth grade, only my second African American teacher (my first had been Sister Betty) told my mother in a conference that she couldn't stand me because I was too poised, proper, and pretty. My mother shared this information with me. I presumed the teacher was joking or being sarcastic. In sixth grade, in Master Brody's class, my White best friend called me a nigger. This time, I fully heard and understood the term. I kicked her shin with my wooden clogs, and she kicked me back. We fought. I won. My best friend received a suspension for a couple of days, Master Brody apologized for my best friend's language, and I kept it movin'. My former best friend and I never really spoke again. There wasn't any follow-up with the class—no lessons on hate speech, no apology required from my best friend. So I kept it moving. Later that year, however, I shaved off my eyebrows when one of my African American classmates at my Quaker school told me that I reminded him of Ernie from *Sesame Street*.

These experiences constituted the third and fourth rungs of my educational ladder toward self-understanding. I was starting to conclude that White girls just didn't like me, Black teachers despised me, and Black boys didn't appreciate me. I was in the eye of a perfect storm. Xavier entered into my life when I turned twelve years old. You already know how that ended. The next rung was shaping into Lucifer: self-hatred. School plays a significant role in a child's life. Irreversible identity formation can gain traction from school experiences. Multiple traumas can lead to expressions of internal and external hatred, depression, anxiety, doubt, fear, anger, revenge, insecurity, jealousy, and a host of other problems. Given the table, the place setting, and the characters, schools can determine the outcome of a child's life. Luckily for me, I had two loving, highly involved parents and grandparents who monitored every invitation I received to sit down at any table.

- **What do you say if your Harvard-educated English teacher threatens to fail you?**

At my new Quaker school, most of my teachers presented a caring attitude and a willingness to help me develop my skills. For most of my high school career, I avoided taking classes with a particular English teacher who was notorious for failing students and who had the reputation of teaching the most difficult books and assigning challenging projects. And to make matters even worse, she had graduated from Radcliffe College, the female liberal arts college affiliated with the all-male Harvard College at the time. No way was I taking any of her courses. Wrong. I was assigned to Teacher Evelyn's course on Charles Dickens. When I looked at her course syllabus and saw *Bleak House* (912 pages) on the lengthy list of required readings, I went to my school counselor and told him to get me out of this course. He proceeded to tell me that the English Department had noticed that I was not signing up for more challenging curricula, and it appeared that I had targeted Teacher Evelyn as the teacher to avoid. Therefore, I was going to take this course as my required English class for high school graduation.

Teacher Evelyn was a White, petite, brilliant, high-paced, no-nonsense, by-the-book teacher who, quite frankly, scared me to death. After open-house night, my dad told me that Teacher Evelyn scared even him. I thought, *Are they kidding me? If my dad, who is brilliant, has some trepidations about my English teacher, I will never pass this class.* I couldn't believe that my English teachers had ganged up on me and figured out my game plan to graduate high school with a low-maintenance kind of brain food. I didn't want any additional stress in my life, especially in my favorite subject. The course began with a personal narrative assignment. Teacher Evelyn wanted to "get to know us" more on a personal level. I splattered together some words and sentences and handed in the assignment. It had taken me about fifteen minutes to complete the essay. Keep in mind that I knew this was a low-level assignment, and it didn't count toward a grade anyway. When she returned my paper with red ink splayed all over my work, I saw the comment "See me." Not a "please see me," just "see me." This tug-of-war between us—my splattered words and her splayed red ink—went on for about two months. She kept sending home warning notices to my parents about my superficial and lame attempts on written assignments. I thought, *I am just fine because I am passing, and this is all that matters.* My mom and dad were science and math experts, so they didn't know how to help me, and I just kept telling them, "I will be fine. I will make my papers longer; she wants longer papers." But Teacher Evelyn wanted scholarship, and she demanded it from every student, especially from me for some reason.

Well, the longer series of splattered words and sentences must have been the tipping point for Teacher Evelyn. She pulled me aside as I was attempting to leave her class, closed her classroom door, and asked me to sit back down in a chair. Remember, she was a by-the-book and no-nonsense teacher. Before I could place my derriere in the chair, she said, "I am going to fail you." Just like that—no warning, no preparation, no other advisory words as a precedent. I couldn't believe it; my worst nightmare was coming to fruition. I knew that I was going to fail this class. I had the audacity to say, "But Teacher Evelyn, I haven't received any failing grades. Why are you going to fail me?" She responded, "If you keep writing these vague papers with no topic development or supporting evidence, you will start receiving failing grades on every assignment." Then she dismissed me.

I knew that I was capable of meeting her expectations, and Teacher Evelyn knew that I was capable of meeting her expectations. She had permitted my splattered words and sentences for a short season; she probably had been giving me some wiggle room to get adjusted to her style of teaching. But her style required excellence from me; her style wanted me to exert my best effort; her style demanded precision; her style reflected confidence in me. Guess what? I exerted my best effort on every subsequent assignment, and I stopped writing those vague papers filled with mediocrity. Teacher Evelyn's Charles Dickens course proved to be the best class I had ever taken in my high school career! I received all A's and B's from her thereafter. She influenced who I became and catalyzed my major in college: English. I cared deeply for Teacher Evelyn. One of my final papers focused on the education of Pip and Estella in *Great Expectations* with a twist of personal reflection on my education. One of Teacher Evelyn's comments on my paper read, "Simply extraordinary, Debra. I think you should tell your story to the world." My White, petite, brilliant, high-paced, no-nonsense, by-the-book teacher Evelyn escorted me all the way to the top of my educational ladder toward self-understanding. I was no longer scared to soar beyond the expectations that I had established for myself. I was so proud! Healing had begun ...

- **How would you react if a member of your ethnicity said you didn't belong?**

... or so I thought. It was my freshman year of college, and I was looking forward to new paths and fresh beginnings. I had cut a deal with my parents, mostly with my dad. If I lived at home and commuted to college, he would buy me a car. I really wanted to live in a college dormitory, but having my very own wheels would present opportunities for freedom and independence. I took the deal, but I got hoodwinked because I didn't get a car until my sophomore year. And I received the privilege of a car only after I pressured my dad every day to buy a car, saying otherwise I would drop out of school. My dad and I have always had a push-me, pull-me relationship. We argued constantly because we are so much alike; we can be obstinate and quite tactical.

Even though I was a commuter, I wanted to still be involved with campus life. So I searched for clubs and activities to which I could belong. I joined the debate club, the newspaper staff, and the minority student union. My interest in the newspaper declined because it became too much work to keep up with the homework and projects for my college classes and also write full-length articles for a club. The minority student union really sparked my interest because I thought the group would be supportive and empowering. I was so naive and too eager to please folks in power.

I attended my first meeting of the minority student union in mid-October, I think. The faculty sponsor was a tall, fairly plump Black woman whose raspy voice seemed to indicate that her breathing might be compromised by her weight. I never saw her smile, and she never spoke to me when I waved to her on campus. She seemed angry with the world, which I could partially understand at the time. But why was she angry with me? In the first meeting, the group's president indicated that some leadership positions would be vacant, and he wanted to take names of people who would be interested in running for a particular office. I volunteered to run for an office. Yes, I was a freshman in college in her first club meeting with college sophomores, juniors, and seniors, and I had the audacity to think I might serve as a good leader. Since I had done so well with Teacher Evelyn, receiving an A– in an English class taught by a Harvard graduate, perhaps I thought I was a "boss" student. Who knows. Nonetheless, I put my metaphorical hat into the race.

Well, at the end of the meeting, the faculty sponsor—I will call her Donna—called me over. She said that she would like to speak with me in her office and asked if I could walk there with her. Excited and curious, I answered that of course I would walk with her to her office. When we arrived, I admired the beautiful mahogany woodworking surrounding the room; her office looked like she, an African American professional woman in a world of White male privilege, had finally "moved on up" just like the Jeffersons, George and Weezie. Her university position and rank instilled hope and inspiration. After I sat down deeply into the red velvet–cushioned chairs, she moved behind her massive mahogany desk, placed both of her hands and knuckles onto the desk while remaining standing, and said, "Who do you think you are? Do you think you are Black? You don't dress Black, you don't act Black, and you don't even talk Black. I would like you to write me an essay on what it means to be Black in America." Just like that—no warning, no preparation, no other taunting words as a precedent. My mind slowly detached from my body, and I thought, *Is this real? Where am I? What's happening?* I stared blankly into her face and her piercing eyes. I started to cry, then bawl, which progressed to wailing while doubled over into my arms and then onto her mahogany desk. Donna softened her demeanor just enough to offer me a box of tissues without any follow-up words of comfort. I eventually gathered my shoulder bag of books and my umbrella and exited her office, after promising her that I would hand in the essay. She said some other foul things that I am choosing not to include.

I never wrote the essay, and I never returned to the minority student union. I kept it movin'. But I had difficulty looking into the faces of my fellow African American students on campus because I presumed they knew about my office visit with Donna. I eventually learned that she never discussed our meeting with anyone. Years later, I also learned that she had been fired from the university because of a drug addiction. She died a few months after she was fired. Donna compounded my traumatic experiences with Black women (Sister Betty and the teacher from my Quaker school). Unfortunately, after I had been teaching for several years and was a seasoned veteran, my life intersected with another Donna who attempted to destroy my spirit. But I had learned from my parents and John Milton that the mind is owned by the self, and I could choose to make a hell out of heaven and a heaven out of hell.

- **How would you feel if you publicly received comments on your hair and wardrobe every day?**

My hair and clothing arrive in a room before I do. "Debra, what did you do to your hair? It seems longer. Is it a different color?" "Did you get a haircut or something?" "Is that all of your hair?" "Boy, your hair is poofy today." These are a small sample of the opening comments from White colleagues when I enter their presence after I've done something "different" with my hair. Or I receive comments like "Why do you dress up for work so much? Who are you trying to impress?" or "Did you get that dress on sale? Because I saw that exact dress at Saks Fifth Avenue. Where do you shop for your clothes?" If I really want to exasperate and baffle the onlookers, I might actually arrive in a room and ask, "Do you like my hair?" when I am wearing a brand-new outfit, yet my hair hasn't changed at all.

I am exhausted from the attention. Most people don't realize that my hair houses some painful memories. When White people fetishize Black hair, it rouses a Lucifer moment. My racial identity lives within a secure and highly guarded facility, and I choose who gets the keys to unlock it. My layered history has not been well known because my privacy has protected my vulnerabilities. I have too many lived experiences with ugliness. I grew up in the late 1960s, the '70s, and the '80s. I didn't play with dolls that looked like me; I didn't see Hollywood actresses who looked like me and were considered beautiful. My world of make-believe consisted of a white, yellow-haired Baby Alive who ate powdered applesauce, drank fake milk, and defecated a watery substance into her diapers. When I turned eight years old, I finally received the prized White Barbie doll with all of her trimmings. My Barbie had fancy dresses and coats, high-heeled shoes, and a stage that turned her unresponsive existence into a rotating and revolving fantasy of my mind. Yes, I did have a happy childhood slipping into an unknown world of Whiteness, a place of quiet privilege for a private Black child of extremely hardworking parents.

Despite the unconditional love and warmth that enfolded me in the strong arms of an extended family home, my parents and maternal grandparents could not dispense self-love. In fact, no individual person can hand self-love over to another human being. The journey toward self-love is directed and completely orchestrated by each individual person. I didn't arrive in the world loving myself. I looked for self-love in the movies; I looked for self-love among my playmates; I looked for self-love in the clothing stores; I looked for self-love in magazines; I looked for self-love in hair salons. I just never found it on the movie screen, the face of a friend, the lifeless model, or the beauty shop. Even in my neighborhood hair spots, when I got my hair "did," it just didn't measure up to White hair. I have always wondered if self-love is taught somewhere. Do people learn about it in school or at home? Am I the only one who was absent on the day it was taught? Since I saw and knew some people who had it, I presumed something must be wrong with me. As a child, I hadn't acquired the sophisticated skill of looking into the faces and actions of my parents and grandparents to see if they possessed it. I just knew that my best friend Stacey had long auburn hair with matching freckles and walked like a breeze and talked proudly about herself.

Stacey always asked if I wanted to brush her hair and style it. Of course, I obliged her by taking her Conair hairbrush and gently pulling her hair to the back of her head and shoulders, brushing her hair with long slanted strokes. At least one hundred strokes were necessary so that Stacey could keep her hair healthy and silky—"and please make sure that your hands are clean and not sticky," she counseled me. She would often close her eyes and soften her demeanor as I brushed her hair and braided it into pigtails or a French braid. *Yes*, I thought, *Stacey has self-love*. One

24

time, I arrived early to school with my solid wooden soft-bristled brush and my Goody barrettes, ready for my one hundred strokes toward styled, silky, and healthy hair too! Stacey said, "Ew, your hair is too greasy and rough. I can't let you use my brush." When I proudly showed her that I had brought my own brush, thereby indicating we could progress toward "doing" my hair, she turned and walked away from me. About a week later, I noticed that Stacey had found another friend to love her hair.

I remember telling my mom, "Stop putting that Ultra Sheen green grease gunk in my hair" and "Straighten my hair with an electric comb, not the hot comb on the stove." Luckily for me, my mom, a pediatric nurse practitioner, always chose moments like this to teach me some racial pride. She gently explained that our hair was different than the hair of White people. She further explained that Black hair was normally very dry and fragile and could easily break without good moisture, and the Ultra Sheen was used to give the hair moisture. Okay, this made sense to me, but I still wanted her to use an electric comb to straighten my hair. She emphatically insisted that if she honored my request, I wouldn't have any hair. I actually took a brief moment to consider the option of not having any hair at all. I am glad that I had "the God-given sense," to borrow a phrase from my poppop, to listen to my beautiful and loving mother.

I still don't understand why folks are so curious about our hair. Why does a new "do," as we call it in my community, need an explanation, a pronouncement, or a rationale for its existence? My hair is a sacred place—it houses my joys and sorrows, it keeps my secrets, it awards me laughter on some days, and sometimes it gives me love. Forgive me if I choose not to share its mystery with you. If I unfold its tale to you, a part of me dies. My hair has been fried, burned, permed, and weaved to look like yours so that I could be loved by you. But "when I was a child, I spake as a child, I understood as a child, I thought as a child: but when I became a [woman], I put away childish things" (1 Corinthians 13:11 KJV).

...w my hair is an accessory and extension of my beauty and identity. If I choose to braid it, I am making a statement. If I choose to straighten it, I am making a statement. If I choose to cut it off entirely, I am making a statement. If I choose to wear a wig, I am making a statement. If I choose to weave in colors, highlights, jewels, and other textures, I am making a statement. Sometimes I accessorize to suit my purpose and audience. Indeed, my hair is my crown of glory; its power and legitimacy do not crave watchful eyes and curious, unfamiliar hands. I try to wear it proudly because that's just my style, and I don't think my style is anyone's business. I fully embrace a delightful comment on my style; otherwise, please keep it movin'.

One day, a White colleague and friend walked up to me and placed both of her hands down into my hair without saying a single word. I thought of Stacey. A Lucifer moment surfaced. I wished that she had kept it moving because self-hatred looked me in the eyes again. My *childish* thoughts resurfaced.

- **How would you feel if a person in power searched your belongings and your person in front of others without legal authority?**

The teaching profession has always awarded me moments of glory and moments of defeat. It is the one profession that mimics the roller-coaster ride of life brilliantly. My early years as a teacher captured a passionate, demanding young woman ready to change the world student by student. My middle years as a teacher reflected a passionate, demanding woman ready to change the world student by student with a new style of freedom. I moved into a greater understanding of the political system within my district, and I chose to knead the system so that my students were never compromised by it. I followed the rules, but I discovered ways around administrivia. Schools have become places of business, not places for learning. Seemingly, it is more important for me to take attendance by a designated time than it is to counsel or console a student in emotional pain. It is more important for me to check boxes, submit forms, answer all emails within twenty-four hours, return telephone calls within twenty-four hours, resolve parental conflicts immediately, attend meetings, listen to the constant ebb and flow of announcements over the loudspeaker during instructional time, report to class coverages for absent colleagues, complete disciplinary forms, monitor study halls, check hall passes, distribute paperwork, report to assigned duties and tasks, collect canned and boxed foods, monitor student additions and subtractions from my courses, submit grade-change forms, transfer grades from students who transfer into my courses, transfer grades for students who leave my course, chaperone students in assemblies, go over schedule changes, huddle in a corner with my students during a lockdown drill, go outside during a fire drill, listen for my name called over the loudspeaker, and do other innumerable tasks than it is for me to *teach*. Administrators visit classrooms to evaluate a teacher once per year. The evaluation period lasts about ten to fifteen minutes, whereas whole-class instruction lasts fifty to fifty-five minutes. So I incorporated my own strategic plans to make sure my students thrived academically and emotionally, despite the distractions of the business. I learned how to cope within a system in desperate need of rehabilitation and resuscitation. American schools need healing. In my middle years, I learned how to function within an educational trauma unit. As I moved into a more seasoned space, I downshifted into a still passionate, still demanding freedom flyer who earned respect.

In the state of Pennsylvania, standardized testing occurs at certain moments of the academic year, and prior to proctoring and supervising these tests, PA teachers must complete a certain number of hours of an online training course. The training is supposed to protect the integrity of the tests and ensure students perform to the best of their abilities. Administrators assume a pressure-cooker type of role and therefore a dictatorial stance; they must guarantee that all tests are monitored properly and returned to the state without any missing tests or answer sheets. The entire process and system remind me of Katy Perry's song and music video "Chained to the Rhythm"—folks blankly staring, stoic, running around and around in a hamster wheel, fulfilling a duty without a heartbeat. It's school, not education.

On test day, my and my fellow proctor's day began with not having all of the students for our session in attendance; a couple of students were absent, and we had a test and answer sheet for a student who was not on our master list. It is important to reveal that all of my school administrators at the time were White males, and my colleague and I belonged to different minority groups. Prior to the start of testing, I called the appropriate school extension to inform the appropriate school administrator that there was an extra test and answer sheet for a student not included on my master list. The secretary took my information, and I walked the extra test and answer sheet over to the correctly assigned classroom teacher proctor, also a White male.

After the lengthy test was finished and materials were gathered and returned, the madness and wreckage to my heart began. A student's test and answer sheet were missing. I was already immersed in my instructional plan with my first-period class when I got a telephone call asking for the missing test and answer sheet. I explained that I didn't have any more tests and sheets. I returned to teaching my lesson. Approximately fifteen minutes later, I received another call asking for the same information; the caller wanted to know if I was absolutely sure that I didn't have the test. I provided the same response. The caller/secretary was recalling a previous year's event when I had locked a student's test and answer sheet in my classroom closet because no administrators were available to receive it and I needed to pick up my daughter from school. The state rules had been less authoritarian in previous years. I returned to teaching my lesson.

The class ended, and I checked my email messages and noticed that I had several emails inquiring about the missing student test and answer sheet. I promptly responded to the emails with the same response as the two telephone calls.

Forty minutes later, the administrator's secretary, who was also White, arrived in my room asking about the same test. I responded with the same answer. Without asking, she proceeded to look through my desk drawers and search on top of my classroom shelves for the test. My next class was patiently waiting for me to begin teaching while watching the search party, but I was waiting for the secretary to finish searching the premises. She left. I began teaching. Approximately fifteen minutes later, I heard my name called on the loudspeaker; I was being asked to call the office. I stopped teaching to call the office. The administrator on the phone wanted to know if I had the missing student test and answer sheet, and would I please double-check my things and classroom to make sure that I didn't have the missing items? No need to do this, I explained. I didn't have the missing items. I returned to teaching. Approximately one hour and thirty minutes later, the administrator interrupted my third class for the day by physically entering my room and then checking my desk drawers, closet, pocketbook, and bookbag without permission and in front of my students. One of my students said aloud, "Wow, Dr. Hobbs, what they got you for? Do they think you packing?" I explained to my students that there was a student test and answer sheet missing, and they thought I had it. After a comprehensive search of my classroom desk and drawers, cabinet tops, closet, purse, and bookbag, the administrator left. I returned to teaching.

My Lucifer moment had arrived, clutching humiliation, anger, resentment, embarrassment, misery, disappointment, and perceived racism for dance partners. After more than twenty years of my teaching in the district, my seasoned status had met chaos. By the end of the day, I was truly not feeling well physically. As I attempted to sit down to gather my thoughts quietly, I got an idea.

I walked over to a colleague to ask if he had the missing student test and answer sheet; he did. The test that was missing was the test I had given to my colleague earlier that morning, the one I had received in error. I asked if my colleague would accompany me downstairs to the administrator's office and validate what had happened. The administrator was not there, and his secretary, who had called me twice and searched my classroom, was on her way out of the door. We explained to her the details of the confusion, and she grabbed the student test and answer sheet from my colleague's hands and yelled at me publicly in front of listening students and adults. She turned to go back into her office area to lock up the test and then walked out. I remained in the hallway, staring blankly into the eyes of my colleague, who offered no words of comfort. Then he walked away and went into the main office. I remained in the hallway briefly, staring at the walls, and then walked back upstairs alone, packed my school bag, and drove to pick up my daughter from school. This fiasco with two White men and a White female secretary reeked of racism. I learned that the same treatment had been given to the other teacher who belonged to a minority group as well, except she hadn't been yelled at publicly by an administrative secretary. A piece of my heart broke that day because I had previously had wonderful professional and friendly relationships with the administrator, secretary, and colleague. The secretary did later formally apologize for yelling at me. Given my layered history with White men and intergenerational trauma, I felt another betrayal, another surprise rejection, another receipt of a "you don't matter" message. My heart doesn't ache as much as it used to in regard to this situation; however, it still needs to heal.

- **Suppose you were formally escorted by a security officer, who is a former police officer, to your boss's office?**

American schooling is designed for war. The architectural design of school buildings, regardless of whether they are public or private, copies the architectural design of prisons. They are low-level, often cinder block or concrete block buildings, with few windows and entrances, low-bid fixtures, and neutral gray- or white-colored facades and walls. They have clanging bells and buzzers; hallways constructed for tailored, controlled mass movement; flat roofs; gates and fences; high-positioned lighting to check on the inmates; security guards pacing the internal and external yards, entrances, and exits; an open cafeteria with fold-up tables and chairs; assigned duties; rules and regulations; penalties for nonconformity; a health suite; a correctional/detention center for discipline problems; lockdown drills; seclusion rooms; wardens/assistant principals; cells called classrooms; surveillance cameras; staff patrols; water fountains; exercise rooms; and managerial/correctional staff and faculty. And inmates must ask for permission for bathroom and movement privileges. I understand an administrator's viewpoint: they want compliance; they need order; they demand respect; they impose control in order to maintain order and respect. It is the nature of their job, unfortunately. However, when a White male administrator uses the aforementioned viewpoint unreasonably on me— an African American female, professional, veteran, respected, educated teacher with a layered history with White males and intergenerational trauma—a Lucifer moment erupts.

My day began as usual. I parked the car, walked to the teacher sign-in location, signed in, and greeted students and other folks in the hallways as I traveled to my third-floor classroom. There I opened the door, settled in to the morning routine by placing items in the closet and sitting down to review lesson plans, and greeted my first-period class. After teaching my first-period class, I was sitting down to respond to email messages when there was a knock on my classroom door. It was one of the school's White male security guards, who was also a dear friend. We always loved to chat about our Eagles football team; we especially loved to engage in friendly banter about the Cowboys football team as well.

However, this visit was a disciplinary one. After some friendly greetings, my friend the security officer told me that he was there to escort me to Mr. Smith's office (Mr. Smith was also a White male). I responded, "Are you kidding me? Why? Am I a threat to the school or something?" My friend the security officer said, "I am not really sure. I think it pertains to an email or something like that."

We continued to talk as I was escorted down the hallway by the security officer. I said, "Are you serious? I am being escorted to Mr. Smith's office because of an email?" He responded, "I think so." At this point, my anger was seething because my image and character were being tarnished in front of others. I began to think, *I am being humiliated and demeaned for an email? I wonder how many other teachers have been escorted to Mr. Smith's office for an email infraction. I wonder how many White teachers have been escorted by a security guard to Mr. Smith's office. I have been a veteran teacher in the district for twenty-eight years at this point. Is this the first time a teacher has been escorted? Why me? Is a Black female teacher being used to make some point? This is just great. I am being paraded through the hallways like a common criminal before my African American students, who need role models, people who look like them and have achieved something in this White-washed world. My White students need role models too. Now they think I have done something horrible. I am sure some of them think all Black people are criminals—here is just another one who has been masking herself as a good person.* These were just some of my thoughts that day.

Upon arriving at Mr. Smith's office, I was asked to take a seat and wait until Mr. Smith was ready to speak with me. I learned that I was being treated in this way because I hadn't responded to an email that had been sent to me Sunday evening. It was now Monday morning, around 9:00 a.m. I guess one of the wardens had declared war on me that day.

The preceding stories constitute a tiny sampling of my personal experiences with race in American education, which include private, public, and parochial classrooms and undergraduate and graduate universities. As both an African American student and an African American teacher, I found that these painful realities forced me into Lucifer moments. Contending with all of these scenarios fueled fear, rage, and confusion. But more often than not, my self-condemnation suffocated my breathing. Eric Garner's murder didn't suddenly usher in a keen awareness and comprehension of Black asphyxiation; a state of asphyxia is part of the walk of life for every African American hoping and praying to survive the hunt. I am grateful, at least, that the hunters have begun to awaken to the lethal consciousness of our existence. Perhaps the awakening might, ultimately, confirm and affirm the reality of Black lives.

CHAPTER 4

Trauma, Part Two

I come as one but stand as ten thousand.
—Maya Angelou

THE SITUATION WITH Xavier provided a fundamental platform on which I stood. I do not have a degree in psychology, but I imagine that I would be a quick study. Consider the circumstances: middle-class, African American Christian female in a racially divided country falls for a guy from the privileged side of the tracks who originates from a wealthy Jewish family; guy and girl profess their love for one another secretively; an upcoming annual black-tie social gala presents an opportunity for the secretive relationship to be formally announced; guy dumps girl to take a more socially acceptable mate. Okay, perhaps I am being a bit melodramatic. But this scenario is not new, is it? You have probably read it, or at least seen it, before—yes, *Romeo and Juliet*, *West Side Story*, *Aida*, Cleopatra and Mark Antony, or any young adult film on *Netflix* these days. The details of the stories may be slightly different, but the theme is the same: tragic love stories. My story, thank goodness, didn't end tragically, but it did leave me with some residual issues associated with trusting White men. This experience is layered with my knowledge and understanding of Thomas Jefferson and Sally Hemings; the condoned rapes of Black women perpetrated by White male slave owners; the public exhibitions of whippings staged by White male slave owners; White society's visual depictions of Black women as robust mammies with big red mouths, their hair wrapped in headscarves; the lynching of Black women by White male lynch mobs from 1880 to 1930; the rape of Recy Taylor by six White men in 1944; the disproportionate number of Black female homicides committed by men (either White or Black)—more than three times the number of homicides of White women[7]—and a judicial, political, and cultural system that ignores the worth of Black women.

There are layers of history activated in my adult mind every day; a simple disagreement with a White male can spark an avalanche of mental anguish, activate the limbic brain, and catalyze my reliving of my surprise rejection from Xavier and my total humiliation. Then I begin my dance with Lucifer. The dance is not elegant; it is not chic. It is self-hatred. Depending on the trauma and the layers of history, a Lucifer moment can turn inward in the form of self-hatred, or it can turn outward in the form of racist thinking, which has the potential to develop into racist behavior. Can you imagine if I never experienced any positive encounters with White males along my life's journey—if that was added to my knowledge and understanding of White males throughout history and my viewing of the media coverage of Black women and men and my memory of Xavier? Well, the resulting Lucifer dance could be either self-annihilation (inward) or White male annihilation (outward). Simply speaking, I would hate myself, or I would hate white males. Certainly, these destructive options couldn't possibly get any worse. Wrong.

Eckhart Tolle, with the help of groundbreaking research in the field of epigenetics, explores the role of intergenerational transmission of trauma.[8] Tolle writes, "The remnants of pain left behind by every strong negative emotion that is not fully faced, accepted, and then let go of join together to form an energy field that lives in the very cells of your body."[9] This "pain-body," as Tolle calls it, is basically a collective warehouse of all the pain suffered throughout the history of humanity and grows daily as it collects and stores our pain. Therefore, every child born enters the world with an emotional burden already housed in his or her DNA. Scientific studies reveal converging evidence supporting the idea that offspring are affected by parental trauma exposures occurring before their birth, and possibly even prior to their conception. The concept of intergenerational trauma acknowledges that exposure to extremely adverse events impacts individuals to such a great extent that their offspring find themselves grappling with their parents' post-traumatic state. A more recent and provocative claim is that the experience of trauma—or more accurately the effect of that experience—is "passed" somehow from one generation to the next through non-genomic, possibly epigenetic mechanisms affecting DNA function or gene transcription.[10]

Although scientific perspectives on the effects of trauma on future generations are still evolving, the early studies prove significant connections. Bezo, a doctoral psychology student at Carleton University in Ottawa, conducted a qualitative pilot study of 45 people from three generations of 15 Ukrainian families: those who had lived through the Holodomor [the mass starvation of millions of Soviet Ukrainians from 1932 to 1933, considered by many to be an intentional genocide orchestrated by Joseph Stalin's regime], their children and their grandchildren. People spontaneously shared what they saw as transgenerational impacts from that time, including risky health behaviors, anxiety and shame, food hoarding, overeating, authoritarian parenting styles, high emotional neediness on the part of parents and low community trust and cohesiveness—what many described as living in "survival mode."[11]

Other researchers around the world are conducting and piloting studies on the intergenerational effects of the Holocaust, the Khmer Rouge killings in Cambodia, the Rwandan genocide, the displacement of American Indians, and the enslavement of African Americans. The transgenerational effects are not only psychological, but also familial, social, cultural, neurobiological, and possibly even genetic, according to researchers.[12]

Now let's revisit May 25, 2020, to see if you can see what I saw. I sat down on my all-white fabric couch, surrounded by comfort, and picked up my cell phone to check out the worldview via Twitter. I discovered some disturbing postings regarding yet another situation between a White police officer and a Black man named George Floyd. I decided to investigate the buzz regarding the "death." I put down my phone and picked up my iPad so that I could view the cell phone recording of the event for myself on a larger screen.

I see two White police officers surround a van: one is on the passenger's side, and the other goes to the driver's side of the van. I think to myself, *Why are they taking so long with the driver (who is not in view)? What is the officer doing to the driver? I can't see.* I watch the driver's side officer pull George Floyd, dressed in a black undershirt and dark pants, out of the vehicle. Floyd staggers almost pigeon-toed toward the sidewalk while the White officer pushes him from behind. Floyd is handcuffed. I think, *Wow, this guy Floyd seems totally incapacitated. He can barely walk, and his feet are turned inward, and his shoulders are slumped and bent forward. So why is he handcuffed? He needs help walking. Did they formally charge him with a crime? Did they read him his rights before they handcuffed him?* As another police car arrives, Floyd is forced into a downward sitting position on the sidewalk, and he grimaces in pain. I think, *What did this guy do? He seems to be in total compliance because he is too weak to resist or put up a fight despite his stature. Are the handcuffs too tight? Because this guy is grimacing in so much pain.* The third officer gets out of his vehicle and just stares at the other two officers, who are engaged in conversations. I think, *What is that first police officer saying to some woman, and why did she pass him something and he place it in his pocket? Why is the third police officer needed? The guy, George Floyd, is not putting up a fight. It looks like he can hardly stay upright in a seated position.*

Floyd's officer is seemingly interviewing Floyd and writing something down on a notepad, while Floyd, still seated, is slowly falling over sideways on the cement sidewalk. I think, *Are they going to call for some medical assistance for this man? And what has he been charged with? Why is there so much lingering time, with the passenger's side police officer talking with a woman and the third police officer just staring at the other two police officers? Are they going to formally place him in a police vehicle? What the heck are they doing to him, and for what?* After a period of time, Floyd's officer shows officer 3 the notepad. Officer 3 takes the notepad back to his vehicle and gets in his vehicle. He drives forward slightly while Floyd's officer yanks Floyd into a standing position and walks Floyd across the street. Meanwhile, Floyd is still grimacing in pain. I wonder, *Why are they now walking this teetering man across the street? This is too much posturing and prolonging to be a legitimate arrest. Do these officers know what they are doing? Are they waiting on somebody or something? There are three police vehicles on the scene, and they haven't placed him in a single one yet. Why not? I know a lot of police officers, and this situation seems out of control. I know the elements of a lawful arrest, detainment, and search and seizure; I have friends and family in law enforcement. Are they trying to flaunt their power and just draw in a crowd to scare Black people?*

Floyd is forced, staggering and pigeon-toed, across the street, and officer 3 drives his vehicle across the street. Then Floyd falls to the ground. I think, *Where is the guy that they handcuffed? I can't see him anymore. What are they doing to him?* Then another police officer (Chauvin) pulls up in his vehicle, and three officers are seen restraining Floyd, with one officer holding a knee on Floyd's neck. The officer with his knee pressed into Floyd's neck also has a gloved hand shoved into his own pocket while Floyd moves his chest, attempting to maneuver his shoulders and chest up, begging, "Please let me stand. Ah, ah, ah, ah [deep guttural sounds]. I can't breathe. Ah, ah, ah, you're killing me." I think, *Oh my god, I can now hear the guy begging for his life. Why is the officer with his knee on Floyd's neck slightly smiling while keeping his gloved hand in his pocket? This is absolutely sickening. The officer with his knee on Floyd's neck is enjoying his conquest of a brawny Black man. This is just another reenactment of* Mandingo. *I am going to throw up. Master police officer has won himself another darky for his trophy case.*

I hear a citizen say to the officers, "Hey, why don't you just put him in the police car? Do you see that blood is coming out of his nose?" The officer with his knee on Floyd's necks says to Floyd, "You know you are resisting arrest, don't you?"

As Floyd struggles to lift himself up to breathe, I watch the police officer's knee begin to bear down even harder on Floyd's neck. After eight minutes and forty-six seconds worth of pressure, Floyd stops moving; his eyes are now closed, and I watch white foam ooze from Floyd's mouth. I think, *Did I just watch an execution before my very eyes? What just happened?* I watch the footage again. I think of lines from Grand Master Flash:

> *Don't push me 'cause I'm close to the edge*
> *I'm trying not to lose my head*
> *It's like a jungle sometimes*
> *It makes me wonder how I keep from goin' under*

Then I watch the footage a third time. I think, *How is my daughter going to survive in this destructive world that hates all of us Black people? I am confused. I don't understand why White folks hate us so much. Our lives have never mattered to them.* I think of words from Grand Master Flash again: "You'll grow in the ghetto livin' second-rate, and your eyes will sing a song called deep hate." I am so sick of the struggle—smiling, laughing, and singing while bleeding out before America's eyes.

Straightaway, my need for hostile clarity encouraged one more look to fuel a war. Lucifer had arrived. I was poised for an angry encounter, a trigger word, or a simple glance or stare from any White person to ignite holy verbal terror. I've got fully activated pain-bodies, twisted DNA, layered history, and a bad attitude. I was ready. You ready?

The most newly released body cam footage permits all of us to now access the actual unedited version with an unobstructed view and clear sound. You will see George Floyd with a frightened face, bent forward in submission and begging as he is pulled out of his vehicle. Prior to being yanked out of the car, Floyd begs for his life, saying, "Oh please, please, please don't kill me. Please don't kill me. I just buried my mother." With this unedited, unobstructed view and clear sound in the newest version, I stopped watching midrecording. No more viewing for me.

I don't believe that my descent into hatred is uncommon. We rarely unpack our own suitcases; all of us are carrying around heavy burdens from the death of a loved one, episodes of extreme disappointment/embarrassment, doubts about our physical appearance or our intellectual capacities, worries about the future, feelings of loneliness and/or isolation, concerns about our children, and a host of even more traumas, like rape, murder, incest, and hatred. When you were overwhelmed with complete boredom in a meeting, did you tell your boss or supervisor that the meeting was boring and why, or did you tell your closest friend and engage in a complaint fest? We are afraid of what we might have hidden beneath the surface of our skin; we never want to appear vulnerable, weak, broken, sad, or angry before our fellow human beings, especially those with power, because we might be perceived as inferior, below par, unhealthy, not at our best, inadequate, and so on. So we would rather mask our true selves with an appearance of fake composure. How many times have you anticipated a "how are you today"? And you quickly respond with "good, good." Or better yet, do you have a packaged, non-engaging response to an anticipated question before the question is verbally stated, and your response isn't even appropriate for the question? But you just keep it moving.

As an African American, I intimately understand Paul Laurence Dunbar's poem "We Wear the Mask." I bet you could too! Our layered histories may be different, our genetic codes may reveal different intergenerational traumas, and our ranks in society could be entirely different, but our shared human condition will forever remain the same.

We wear the mask that grins and lies,
It hides our cheeks and shades our eyes,—
This debt we pay to human guile;
With torn and bleeding hearts we smile,
And mouth with myriad subtleties.
Why should the world be over-wise,
In counting all our tears and sighs?
Nay, let them only see us, while
We wear the mask.
We smile, but, O great Christ, our cries
To thee from tortured souls arise.
We sing, but oh the clay is vile
Beneath our feet, and long the mile;
But let the world dream otherwise,
We wear the mask![13]

I grew up in a devout Baptist family; my beloved grandparents were church elders (deacon and deaconess), and my attendance in Sunday school and church every Sunday was an uncontested expectation. I read the King James Version of the Bible, and perhaps like some of you, I memorized all of the classic biblical scriptures, such as John 3:16, Matthew 7:12, Ecclesiastes 3:1–8, and John 11:35, among many others.

I remember one particular Sunday evening in which our pastor, Reverend Dr. Jeremiah A. Wright, came to dinner. We had a specific routine for our Sunday dinners, and I was a bit nervous because I knew that I would be called upon to recite a Bible verse. From my childhood perspective, our pastor was larger than life itself, and I really loved him. He was kind, gentle, serious, and funny, and most of all, he was a brilliant teacher. Most of my friends disliked sitting on the hard, wooden church benches during a sermon; sometimes during a sermon, my best friends and I would pass the time by taking a tally of how many times Dr. Mary H. Wright, the pastor's wife, said "amen" or "say so" or "praise Jesus" or "hallelujah." But most Sundays, I did my best to concentrate on the message and try to apply it to my life. I found my pastor's messages soothing, comforting, and inspiring. So if I forgot my Bible verse at dinnertime, I knew that I would have John 11:35 ready to go: "Jesus wept."

I will never forget that evening because I learned about a woman who had committed adultery. *What is adultery?* I wondered. It sounded like a really fancy thing. There was a long discussion about Jesus going to the Mount of Olives and being questioned about his opinion on this woman who had committed adultery and had been taken "in the very act." I listened intently to the adults at the table discussing this woman's fate. I always loved these moments because I could ask any question of my parents, grandparents (who lived with me), and pastor and get an unabridged and clear answer. After getting my answers, I always felt like I had grown at least five feet taller. After I asked, "What did the woman do?" and received my answer, I had a follow-up question. "What did Jesus do to her?" I learned a new scripture that night: "He that is without sin among you, let him first cast a stone at her" (John 8:7 KJV). The New Living Translation states, "Let the one who has never sinned throw the first stone."

Most of us, I imagine, regardless of religion or denomination or creed, carry around at least one mantra, truth, or noble statement about good, clean, and happy living. John 8:7 adorns my heart because it has always served as a guide for my thoughts and actions. The thought of being a "sinner" just like everybody else not only levels our ranks in society; it also unifies all of humanity. It makes us brothers, sisters, and fellow kinfolk. Nobody is greater than another human being, and nobody is lesser than another human being. Have you considered this notion's implications regarding racists? I hadn't, until now, at this moment in my life.

It is important to note that when pain-bodies are activated, layered histories may surface in the conscious or subconscious mind. If you live your life in an unconscious way, then you may be totally unaware of why you may be suffering from hostile and volatile thoughts; however, if you are living consciously, then you possess the power to identify and name your layered histories and use strategies to defuse your emotional reactions. According to Tolle, conscious living involves staying in the present moment, which ultimately aligns us with our soul's purpose. Therefore, unconscious living moves a person in and out of time emotionally and fuels the egoic mind.[14] However, conscious living is possible only after trauma has been addressed and healing begins.

Most of us spend our lives living unconsciously, just plucking, killing, weeping, mourning, stoning, losing, shredding, hating, and casting away each other.

By the way, at the Sunday evening dinner with my pastor, I never did get an opportunity to share "Jesus wept."

CHAPTER 5

Ego

And he said to them all,
If any man will come after me,
let him deny himself, and take up
his cross daily, and follow me.
—Luke 9:23 (KJV)

Pride goeth before destruction,
and an haughty spirit
before a fall.
—Proverbs 16:18 (KJV)

I SPECULATE THAT hatred of any kind results from some type of trauma, and the ego fuels the trauma, which ultimately engages the limbic brain to relive previous painful experiences. Piaget explained that egocentric children assume that other people share their feelings, reactions, and perspectives.[15] Generally speaking, "whenever you feel superior or inferior to anyone, that's the ego in you."[16]

I say the ego is a nasty little troll and serves as the principal tool of Lucifer, a former angel of great promise whose ego challenged God. Oh, it can don all the magical items of success and happiness. It can have a degree from Harvard, drive a Porsche, and live in Silicon Valley. I apologize if you possess all three of these wonderful symbols of societal success; I have nothing but love for you. I just hope that you are happy. Ego can infiltrate our minds and make us think that material success makes us superior to another person. Ego makes us feel greater than or less than another; ego constantly compares itself to others; ego loves things; ego feels threatened; ego wants power; ego is needy; ego wants to win an argument; ego wants privilege and status; ego draws attention to itself; ego is domineering; ego is reactionary; ego has an insatiable hunger and thirst for more; ego is pride; ego is the opposite of love.

At this point in my life, it concerns me that I spiritually know and understand deeply how every human being is exactly the same, yet I act differently. Remember the Sunday dinner with my pastor and the scriptural lesson on throwing stones—don't throw them, essentially because we are all sinners. Well, I can't help but get excited when I accomplish something that other folks couldn't do. For example, if I finish a book first and discuss a particular passage in a unique way with my book club, I get excited. I was first, and nobody else thought of my idea. I think to myself, *Yes, I am exceptional.* When I achieved a really high GPA in graduate school, I told myself, *You rocked your education.* Please notice I didn't reveal my GPA just now—I am trying to get rid of that ego. But I just drew attention to my progress in trying to get rid of the ego, which is still the ego working—darn! Yes, these seem like harmless expressions of one's ego. But suppose we raise the ante slightly.

Let's incorporate an individual pain-body/personal trauma with some collective trauma from the world,[17] some intergenerational trauma (twisted DNA), and some layered history with a tinge of ego. How is this narrative going to end? Surprisingly, this narrative constitutes the life of most of us.

Suppose your father was German (potential intergenerational trauma), and your mother was Mexican (potential intergenerational trauma), and you already inherited the collective trauma of the world; we are all born with the collective trauma. You have two older sisters and one younger sister. At the age of six, you contract polio, and you are bedridden for nine months (personal trauma). As a result of the polio, your right leg and foot become damaged (personal trauma). One day, while you are on a school bus trip with your boyfriend, the bus gets into a serious accident, and you are impaled by a steel handrail that goes into your hip and comes out the other side; additionally, you sustain several fractures in your spine and pelvis (personal trauma). Eventually, you get married, but your husband has several affairs, including one affair with your sister (personal trauma; layered history). Even though you divorce and remarry your husband, he has always supported your creative talent in art, and you love painting mostly self-portraits (personal trauma, layered history, ego). During your turbulent marriage, you get pregnant (a deep desire) with his child, but you miscarry the child (personal trauma). You finally achieve your first solo exhibition as an artist, but you arrive in an ambulance at your exhibition's opening, surrounded by the "comfort" of a four-poster bed due to chronic health problems. And prior to your solo exhibition, your beloved father dies.[18]

Frida Kahlo did not become a racist! Her life did, in fact, include every element in my hypothesis about racist thoughts and behaviors. However, painting set her free and provided an outlet for self-expression; she began painting during her recovery from the bus accident. Painting gave her a vehicle to express all of her hopes, hurts, desires, frustrations, disappointments, and rages. Artistic expression gave her the gift of healing emotional, physical, and psychological trauma. The primary goal of every school should be to help young people discover their gifts and talents and encourage them to offer their beauty to the world. Developing a child's ego in this manner could keep them safe at night because their gift establishes a sense of purpose; it will reinforce for children that they matter—they were born for a reason, which is to serve a divine purpose. This ego development is called identity. If you have a strong sense of identity, the nasty little troll ego dissolves because self-love is born. Racists don't have self-love! This shift for schools will require a new consciousness. If you want to eradicate racism, begin with the children. And the children will follow selfless leadership and administration.

Kahlo's emotional narrative is worth noting because the trauma in this artist's life highlights the varying traumatic experiences suffered by all of us. Some of us have an awareness of the trauma and have healthy ways of expressing our pain. Kahlo used art to channel her Lucifer moments. My mommom and her six siblings used to go into the fields of North Carolina and beat two trees named Tom and Ella, which were named for the children's parents, my great-grandparents. My mommom shared the colorful details of these beatings with me when I was a young child. I remember the bark of these old trees as unrelenting, tough, and thorny. Yet the efforts of my mommom and her siblings somehow prevailed against the intractable trees; at least, in my grandmother's childhood eyes, she successfully got Tom and Ella to finally listen to her point of view. Even young children fully understand injustice and seek a cathartic release of pent-up anger. Adults are no different. If we could draw a continuum of trauma, obviously, each and every one of us could be placed on this scale with discrete placements. Lucifer moments loom in the shadows of our existence. Some of us do not have an awareness or a sustainable means for a cathartic release of trauma. Therefore, some of us continually wrestle with circumstances beyond our control. How does this relate to racism?

The Complexity of Racism

Systemic racism in the United States of America promises a life of hatred for African Americans. This promised life lives out its destiny internally, externally, or both.

African Americans not only are suffering from the "normal" and typical examples of strain and stress (e.g., death of a family member or friend, divorce), but they also have layered histories associated with slavery, daily discrimination, systemic racism, intergenerational trauma, and collective trauma ("pain-bodies") that magnify the strain and stress of their existence. When persistent episodes of the murder of your people appear live on cell phones, television screens, and every handheld device, the soul of the people faces destruction. Facing a soul's destruction on a daily basis can ignite uncontrollable rage, extreme depression, insatiable anger, and fear. At this point in my life, I awaken with joy, grateful for another opportunity to expand my spiritual and earthly selves. When I am confronted with another example of hatred toward my people, my pain-bodies, intergenerational and collective traumas, and layered histories are triggered; yet again, a Lucifer moment arises. This Lucifer moment is going to thrust me into an either internal or external form of expression. I am going to hate myself, or I am going to hate the perpetrator who belongs to a group of people who are historically known for acts of hatred against my people. Plain and simple, this is what happens to me when I watch the news. Racism forces an already heavily burdened people into repetitive cycles of suffering with no end point.

So how does this further relate to Frida Kahlo? Suppose you encounter a young African American person, in your classroom or in your daily experience, who has the exact traumatic profile as the artist except for ethnic background, and you know tragic acts of violence against African Americans materialize daily. Suppose the African American person identifies as male or female. Suppose the African American person identifies as a member of the LGBTQ community. Suppose this African American person has cancer. Suppose this African American person is also a victim of rape. Suppose this African American person is from a single-parent home. Suppose this African American person is from a two-parent home of a White dad and White partner. Suppose this African American person was adopted, with unknown birth parents. Suppose this African American person is addicted to drugs. Suppose this African American person has autism. Suppose this African American person hates White people. Suppose this

African American person hates themself. Suppose this African American ... you fill in the blank.

What is going to be your approach? How are you going to weigh your relationship, your conversation, your interaction? Will you continue to read aloud hateful speech captured in seminal and historical literature? Have you developed such a level of comfort to utter trauma-inducing words of another culture? For example, I know that there are many intellectual arguments surrounding the N-word. If you are a White teacher, how can you handle the inflammatory language in Mark Twain's *Huckleberry Finn* in a respectful and compassionate way? The African American community may reject a White teacher's use of the N-word because it conjures intergenerational trauma and/or a Lucifer moment. Should the White teacher ignore the expressed rejection of a community, if the teacher knows how the language affects the mental, emotional, spiritual, and biological spaces of the African American community? Toni Morrison stated that words serve only two purposes: to heal or to kill. My lived experiences have taught me to trust her. If one of my students rejected my use of a cultural word or an inflammatory word belonging to the tragic history of their ethnicity, I would apologize for using the word; I would contact the guardians of my student and apologize for my ignorance; I would research the ethnic and historical significance of the word to previous and current generations. I would seek instructional strategies and techniques that foster emotional healing; I would respectfully ask the student to educate me on ways to soothe the emotional trauma. I would co-construct some academic lessons with my student that meet the expectations of both academic and emotional intelligences. I would dissolve my ego's embarrassment so that my student would always find a safe space and place with me.

I try to remember and remain mindful that my instructional strategy and approach must undergo change constantly. A

reflective teacher/practitioner knows that every year, every course, every class, and every student is a unique case. Over time, a seasoned teacher builds upon previous years of knowledge to design and implement lesson plans that teach, engage, inspire, and heal learners. In other words, some instructional strategies and techniques cannot be recycled each and every year. I have learned to listen to the voices of my kids. They will tell teachers what they need. Sometimes, their needs surface in a story, poem, essay, class discussion, parent conference, administrative directive or legal document. However, the blank stare, the disruptive behavior, the absenteeism, the bandage, the black and blue skin mark, the frightened face, and the silenced voice may reveal their greatest needs of all. Psychological bruises from sustained trauma show up in every classroom around the world, whether the trauma is racial, gender-based, religious, familial, sexual, mental, emotional, spiritual, or physical. So if a student tells me that my word choice, selection, or usage offends them, I believe them. And sometimes my heightened awareness, understanding, and strategy for one student in a particular year may not work for a similar student profile the following year.

All of us, either consciously or subconsciously, reveal our narratives. If we listen to each other, we will hear unique and common themes. If we seek to understand by reserving judgment, we will open doors for meaningful and compassionate conversations. If we could dispel our pride, we would see ourselves in each other. If we discover ourselves in each other, we will find love. Once we find love, we will have found our divine Creator.

As I move closer to retirement, I have learned that humility breeds wisdom. Embarrassing moments on the teaching stage made me a better teacher. Teaching humbles the reflective practitioner. Ego destroys both our humanity and our spirit. Ego will never erase racism! I could recite many sacred and scriptural texts that discuss the virtue of humility. My favorite stems from the writings of Baha'u'llah:

Be unjust to no man, and show all meekness to all men. Be as a lamp unto them that walk in darkness, a joy to the sorrowful, a sea for the thirsty, a haven for the distressed, an upholder and defender of the victim of oppression ... Be a home for the stranger, a balm to the suffering, a tower of strength for the fugitive. Be eyes to the blind, and a guiding light unto the feet of the erring. Be an ornament to the countenance of truth, a crown to the brow of fidelity, a pillar of the temple of righteousness, a breath of life to the body of mankind, an ensign of the hosts of justice, a luminary above the horizon of virtue, a dew to the soil of the human heart, an ark on the ocean of knowledge, a sun in the heaven of bounty, a gem on the diadem of wisdom, a shining light in the firmament of thy generation, a fruit upon the tree of humility.

—Baha'u'llah[19]

So should a White person use the N-word? Should a Black person use the N-word? Since our minds, bodies, and spirits are constantly evolving, is a revisionist interpretation needed to heal our language and behavioral choices?

Let me recommend that you must dissolve your ego, the nasty troll ego that seeks attention, wants to win an argument, feels threatened, proves reactive, condemns others, seeks the "right way" and "my way," and ignores the pain of another. While you dissolve your ego, allow the damaged and broken ego of the African American person to express itself in appropriate ways as much as possible. Don't be frightened by the expression of ego from the African American person because the ego is seeking a safe outlet and haven so that it can heal. Ego expression for an African American is often about identity recognition, not power; since we have a history of being defined as animals and subhuman in both historical and literary texts, we need to be seen, heard, and understood because "when I discover who I am, I will be free."[20] Sometimes the expression of the broken self can be loud, aggressive, hostile, or completely silent and withdrawn. Let me also recommend that you never forget our eternal mindset:

Once riding in old Baltimore,
*   Heart-filled, head-filled with glee,*
I saw a Baltimorean
*   Keep looking straight at me.*

Now I was eight and very small,
*   And he was no whit bigger,*
And so I smiled, but he poked out
*   His tongue, and called me, "Nigger."*

I saw the whole of Baltimore
*   From May until December;*
Of all the things that happened there
*   That's all that I remember.*[21]

I wonder if racists undergo the same mental, emotional, and spiritual distress. Provocative, I know. My students know that I am an advocate of (opening closed conversations.) So let's open one: What makes a person become a racist? I pose the question because babies don't arrive in the world as racists, bigots, and chauvinists. Since I already know and fully believe that no one is greater than or lesser than another person, I am going to move into an interrogative mode, because I have tried to avoid racists and not learn anything about them. Therefore, I don't have an understanding of them. So it is better to pose questions:

- Do you think that as fellow human beings, racists suffer from intergenerational and collective traumas?

- Do you think that racists have layered histories?
  - Do they suffer from a lot of direct and personally negative experiences with African Americans or other groups they hate?
- Is it possible that racists suffer from their own form of self-hatred?
- Is it possible that they suffer from acts of discrimination on a daily basis?
  - Do you think their pain-bodies may be triggered prior to a demonstration or expression of violence against others?

Suppose you encounter a White American person who has lived in dire poverty for an entire lifetime (in other words, poverty has been generational). Suppose you encounter a White American person who has never been able to receive or afford a decent education. Suppose you encounter a White American person who has been the victim of an act of violence perpetrated by an African American. Suppose you encounter a White American person who has experienced several and/or repeated acts of violence perpetrated by African Americans. Suppose this White American person has never experienced any interactions with African Americans other than through the news media. Suppose this White American person has cancer and recently lost their job to an African American. Suppose the White American person was fired by an African American. Suppose this White American person is also a victim of rape. Suppose this White American person is from a single-parent home. Suppose this White American person is from a two-parent home of a Black dad and Black partner. Suppose this White American person was adopted by White supremacist parents, with unknown birth parents. Suppose this White American person hates themself. Suppose this White American ... you fill in the blank.

Resentment and anger can be the effects of any caustic relationship. I am not suggesting that any of the aforementioned scenarios involve caustic relationships unequivocally. I am saying that unhealed trauma can develop into insatiable rage. Depending on the details of who is identified as the victim and who is identified as the aggressor, assailant, or criminal, events can escalate on personal levels. Lucifer moments never discriminate! Once negative energy is absorbed into the heart and mind and continually receives fuel, the outbreak can prove deadly. Think about Mayella Ewell from Harper Lee's novel *To Kill A Mockingbird* or the adapted film, with Gregory Peck playing the role of Atticus Finch. Mayella Ewell, a White American woman, was born into dismal, intergenerational poverty and was raised by an alcoholic, jobless father who raped her. The Ewells use the N-word on a regular basis in their 1930s Maycomb County, Alabama, town. Tragically, Mayella Ewell accuses the innocent Tom Robinson, an employed African American man who brings wages home to his poor but slightly better-living family, of rape. You know the outcome of the trial and verdict: guilty, shot seventeen times in the back as he was trying to flee.

Even though the story is a fictional one, let's see if we can make sense of its painfully realistic plot. We have a White American female who is experiencing the trauma of poverty, inadequate education, and incestuous rape by a racist father, who himself probably resents the Robinsons because they seem better-off than he does. Mr. Ewell is confused by the notion that "all men are created equal" and awarded the "unalienable" right of "Life, Liberty and the pursuit of Happiness" because his life is not representative of the American dream promised. His layered history reveals a number of things: White men previously were slave masters and owners; given his alcoholism, Mr. Ewell may have grown up around intergenerational alcoholic family members as a child; given the town's social strata, the Ewells were probably bullied by the more economically stable White townsfolk; Mr. Ewell doesn't like the fact that Black people who used to be owned by White men are now doing just as well as or even better than him economically. Mayella becomes embarrassed by her friendship with Tom upon her father's discovery of it. The only scapegoat that emancipates the Ewells from internal hatred and constant public embarrassment is Tom Robinson, the mockingbird. The Ewells were invisible to their fellow White citizens of Maycomb County; they were the castaways of society, the fragments of life. The Ewells felt their history and trauma and lived it. Some people can never seem to conquer their plight.

When we encounter people like the Ewells, our humanity needs to show up. We have a moral obligation to not allow hatred to come face-to-face with more hatred. We are all familiar with Martin Luther King's statement: "Darkness cannot drive out darkness: only light can do that. Hate cannot drive out hate: only love can do that." Listen, I am not saying that it is going to be easy. It is hard to look hatred in the eyes and say, *I love you*. However, we must swallow our pride. It is time to learn from our alleged enemies; it is time to understand their emotional narrative and layered history. When Ellison wrote in his novel *Invisible Man*, "I am invisible, understand, simply because people refuse to see me,"[22] perhaps he was indeed speaking, on the lower frequencies, for all of us!

What does a dissolved pride look like in the face of racism?

Do you remember the scene in Alex Haley's *Roots* film when Missy Anne Reynolds (actress Sandy Duncan) says, "I don't likely remember no darky named Kizzy," after asking Kizzy (actress Leslie Uggams), her childhood friend, to give her a drink of water from the fountain? You may recall that Kizzy got the water, secretly spit into Missy Anne's cup of water, and furtively smiled when she saw Missy Anne drink the ruined water. This *is not* a reflection of a dissolved pride! However, when a White Afrikaner boy (Master Harold) spits in the face of his childhood friend and African servant Sam Malapo, Sam conquers his rage and simply takes a handkerchief from his pocket, wipes the sputum from his face, and proceeds to teach the White boy a lesson about love. This *is a* reflection of a dissolved pride! If you get an opportunity to read *Master Harold and the Boys* by South African playwright Athol Fugard, which received the London Critics Circle Theater Award for Best Play in 1983 and a Tony Award nomination for Best Play, you will be able to read the real and true story of Sam Malapo and Master Harold. Fugard wrote this story in an effort to exorcise his demons: his regrets over dehumanizing a man who loved him.

Although it falls outside racial lines, this next example serves as an inspirational story of love, a powerful picture of what I aspire to paint for life. In October 2006, Charles Roberts shot ten Amish schoolgirls in a one-room Amish school in Lancaster, Pennsylvania, before killing himself. On the same day of the shooting, the Amish grandfather of one of the murdered girls expressed forgiveness toward the killer, and the Amish community visited the Roberts family to offer comfort. On the day of the funeral for Charles Roberts, journalists noted that the Amish mourners outnumbered the non-Amish.[23] They did it! The Amish never invited Lucifer into their minds or their hearts. The Amish looked into the face of hatred and said, *I love you.* Honestly, I would like to believe I would respond in a similar manner if confronted with a tragic loss of life.

All families who have lost children experience an irreparable brokenness. How do you find love when hatred surrounds you? How does a person recover from any painful experience? How does anyone look into the face of hatred and harvest love? Well, I have three possibilities: perfect love, love and light wishes, metaphysical/physical hug. The Amish demonstrated the perfect form of love; this is possibility number one. This is the type of love I want from God. I know that my thoughts, words, and actions need to evolve; I know that I make some serious mistakes. But I want to be forever within the embrace of an omniscient, omnipresent, and omnipotent being who loves me regardless of my faults. This is divine love, and I may not be capable of it; clearly, the Amish are capable of it. I am going to strive harder to love those who do not love me. If I fail miserably at loving my enemy, I am going to send love and light wishes to those who hurt me or seek to destroy me. This second possibility is not quite ideal, but I can silently bestow love and light upon another person and truly mean it. Finally, if the first two possibilities seem too complicated, I will choose to hold someone I love in a deep embrace for a period of time in a moment of stillness and silence. Although I may not hold this person in my material and physical reality, I will say their name aloud while physically using my arms to embrace their spirit/essence close to my heart. You can also use a physical hug in reality to express love. If you are courageous, and you have a willing participant, you could achieve benevolence with a hostile person or situation. I was introduced to this possibility when I was having a heated argument with a friend. Rather than continue to engage me in a verbal battle, my friend just grabbed me in a warm embrace and held me tightly for an extended period of time. We held one another in complete silence. My initial shock was quickly replaced by a lowered sense of ego, and I melted almost immediately into a softer disposition. Eventually, I wrapped my arms around him too, realizing my overall stance really didn't matter. In fact, I no longer wanted to argue. Our love for each other in that warm and silent embrace dissipated the heat of conflict. The only thing that mattered was our friendship, despite our differences. This final possibility not only released endorphins within me and my friend; it released positive energy into the universe as well. I know that a physical hug between two arguing friends may not equate with looking hatred in the face and saying, "I love you." But it does allow negative energy to be extinguished from the universe. In fact, all three possibilities release positive energy into the world.

Most of us are deeply concerned about our carbon footprint, but we remain unaware of the dangerous impact of our thoughts on the universe, our environment, and each other. Many first-person accounts of near-death experiences (NDE) convey the tremendous and perilous consequences of our thoughts. The syllogism "beware of your thoughts because they can become your words, and beware of your words because they can become your actions" is truth. Everything we think, say, and do emanates a level of energy into the world. Negative thoughts, words, and actions literally destroy life. If we have 7.8 billion people releasing negative energy into the world via thoughts, words, and actions, then COVID-19 is just the precursor to a more catastrophic possibility. But I believe in our humanity, and in my heart, I believe that our worldwide pandemic is forcing all of humanity into a rebirth. It is a time to be still; it is a time to reflect inwardly and deeply into our souls; it is a time for family; it is a time for reinventing ourselves; it is a time for rebuilding our institutions, especially the structures that have maintained and supported racism; it is a time for forgiveness and new understandings; it is a time to reevaluate our values and beliefs; it is a time for love. It is an ecclesiastical moment.

Even if we can never suppress that troll called ego, to fulfill possibility one or two, we can make this world a place of high vibrational energy. High vibrational levels heal people, Mother Earth, and nations. Have you ever wondered why Earth is the only planet in our solar system without a Greco-Roman god or goddess name?[24] Perhaps "unto whomsoever much is given, of him shall be much required" (Luke 12:48 KJV). Imagine if we expressed our love, at the very least, to those who love us in return—we could improve the health of our world. Perhaps if we did this collectively, we could give hatred no place to roam.

I think John Lennon, with the influence of Yoko Ono, tried to inspire this theme in 1971. We are still evolving as a nation; we are still evolving as human beings; we are still evolving as spiritual souls.

CHAPTER 6

Beauty after Ego Dissolves

IF YOU COME to the literary table with Toni Morrison, be prepared for an exorcism. After reading one of her books, if you haven't received a complete and total purification from all of your demons, then you probably arrived as an uninvited guest. Your presence at her table requires humility, vulnerability, and a herculean desire to learn. When I read or listen to her words, she opens the chambers of my soul. With unprecedented mastery, she does invite special guests to comprehend the lives of African Americans so that her readers discover how dust becomes life. When I teach Toni Morrison's books, I enter a sacred space. My students, both Black and White, enter sacred places with me. Expelling trauma, unmasking counterfeit identity, voicing undisclosed emotion, and achieving liberation are only some of the benefits of our class discussions at Morrison's literary table. Can you imagine *The Bluest Eye*, which centers on a young Black girl's desire for blue eyes, inspiring a White female high school student to gain the courage and bravery to prosecute her father for raping her repeatedly over the course of her childhood, and the father getting sentenced to 805 years in prison?

Can you imagine *The Bluest Eye* unleashing a White male high school student to finally talk openly and publicly about his mother's untimely death from cancer? Can you imagine a young Asian female high school student revealing her family's desire for cosmetic plastic surgery on her eyes to make them rounder and more American? I certainly didn't imagine these scenarios, yet all three are true and real accounts from my classroom teaching experiences with *The Bluest Eye* by Toni Morrison. My students forced me into a place of humility. After establishing critical analytical frameworks, I stepped aside; I stooped down so they could take flight.

I remember distributing the book one year after several introductory exercises on self-image, societal influence, beauty, ugliness, Hollywood, Hitler's Aryan race, and the Holocaust. I have always introduced Morrison carefully, strategically, and compassionately for my students. It is so important to prepare young minds for the secrets she unfolds to the world. Using music, movies, and other signposts from the adolescent world invites my students to Morrison's literary table, helps to bridge the divide, and serves as a staple in my teaching methodology. As I walked around the room, one student, whom I will call Rachel, asked me if she could study a different book with me because she felt that *The Bluest Eye* would be too much for her; she stated that she wanted to remain in the classroom and listen to the discussions on the book, just not read the book. Of course, I immediately accepted her terms. I didn't pressure her or compel her to provide a rationale or explanation. While searching for a worthy alternative reading selection, I continued to guide and instruct my classes with thought-provoking discussions, assessments, and activities. Rachel never missed a single class and proved to be an active and highly engaged student during the entire unit. In fact, about two weeks into the unit, she told me that she wanted to get a copy of the book and read it along with the rest of the class. I was both relieved and excited that Rachel would be joining the journey.

Then one day, Rachel approached me after class and asked if she could speak with me privately about "some things." I immediately provided her a forum because I didn't have another class for the day, and conveniently, she didn't have another class for the day either. The universe aligned for both of us right at that exact moment in time. I closed my classroom door, and she pulled up a chair and sat down next to me. Although Rachel's eyes were hazel-brown, my intuition told me why they appeared "blue" to me. As she began to speak, quite hesitantly at first, looking frightened by what she was about to unfold for the first time, I knew instinctively that *The Bluest Eye* had moved into nonfiction. Out of admiration, respect, and total love for Rachel, I will refrain from retelling the details of her narrative and the grueling emotional, mental, and spiritual process of reliving the trauma. However, I invite you to Morrison's literary table and encourage you to read the story of Pecola and Rachel for yourself. The tale will harrow your soul with unprecedented horror and trauma. Pecola's story ends tragically; Rachel's story ends with emancipation and incarceration. The judicial system cast the statute of limitations to the wind, and Rachel, from the depths of her soul, summoned the courage to prosecute her father for multiple childhood rapes. Her father was sentenced to prison to serve 805 years consecutively, without any opportunity for parole. Rachel declared war and led a crusade against injustice. It gives me pure joy to share that Rachel is happily married, and she and her husband have started a family of their own. Rachel and I share a bond and friendship that has been divinely ordered, in my opinion. We remain in touch, and she still affectionately calls me "Momma Hobbs." If you allow yourself to be led, if you allow change, if you "humble yourselves in the sight of the Lord ... he shall lift you up" (James 4:10 KJV). Miracles do happen!

About ten years after Rachel graduated high school, another miraculous event reshaped my humanity, and my soul grew some more. According to my style of teaching, I begin the academic year with my students wrestling with identity: self-identity, societal identity, familial identity, world and global identities. The literary vehicle of choice, of course, is Toni Morrison's *The Bluest Eye*. In an effort to be more transparent, I engage a purposeful strategy. The adolescent world is riddled with so many perplexing and intense rites of passage that superficiality and authoritative arrogance from a teacher rings the knell of disengagement, disobedience, and disenchantment. So I begin with my vulnerabilities and the mistakes I made in high school. I always have a captive audience. Laying my heart open to a captive audience of teenagers requires trust and faith in them, but the rewards far outweigh the risks. Morrison's book provides the best academic context for me to share my narrative while inviting my young learners to harmonize their hearts with mine. I universalize my African American experience so that my students and I bleed the same red blood—metaphorically speaking, of course. Communal trust, honesty, sincerity, and compassion drive the process.

However, this particular year presented a challenging situation. The class and I were fully immersed in the Morrison unit, yet discussions for one particular class seemed forced, artificial, and hostile. I opened the unit in similar ways to previous years and accomplished the typical team-building and trust-generating activities and assignments. Yet I had one student—let's call him Brutus—who openly confronted me every class period with an antagonistic point of view. So I felt compelled to defend every statement I made and every assignment I gave and to ignore the often-raised hand of Brutus. The situation escalated to the point that his fellow classmates would run into my room and say, "Guess who isn't here today? We can have a good class today with no arguments." I found the entire situation exasperating. I thought, *This White kid absolutely hates me; he must not like Black women or people.* It was the only explanation my limited understanding could summon and the only explanation my ego contemplated. I made the hostile situation all about me; this is what the ego does. Ego feels threatened; ego needs to be right; ego constantly compares self to others; ego is always reactionary; ego always looks to enhance its sense of identity; ego feels diminished; ego is dependent on external factors. I was fully immersed in my ego. If I had changed my reaction to Brutus, I could have changed my reality and our relationship sooner. I was absolutely miserable, wallowing in my own sense of pride. I was concerned about losing power and embarrassed about losing control over our discussions.

I had a certain agenda of life lessons and academic skills that I needed to teach, and this kid was disrupting the entire process. Ego, ego, ego!

One afternoon, I was eating lunch in my classroom by myself, trying to decompress from yet another confrontational day with Brutus. Quite honestly, I wanted to go home and just have a good cry. Another student knocked on my door and opened the door while knocking. I thought to myself, *Oh my goodness, can I just get a moment of peace in this place?* Ego talking again. But I decided to simply go with the flow and hear what this student needed to ask me or tell me or request of me. I am forever grateful to this student, whom we'll call Maxine. Maxine walked softly toward me and pulled up a chair. She sat down, and proceeded to tell me that Brutus had experienced a lot of pain in his life. She told me that he had lost his mother to cancer while he was in the third grade, and she shared how close he had been to his mother. He had never fully recovered from the loss. She advised me to not take Brutus's comments too personally. This is exactly why the ego is a dangerous and extremely destructive force; it severs relationships and draws erroneous conclusions. If I had prevented the student from interrupting "my" lunch, I would have potentially alienated two students: Maxine, who had compassion for me, and Brutus, who simply needed love, patience, understanding, and a safe space to express some deeply rooted trauma.

After reflecting on Maxine's disclosure, I had a clearer, more accurate picture of Brutus in my mind. Brutus always spoke to me in the hallways, with a "Good morning," "Good afternoon," or "Hello." Friendly greetings outside of the classroom aren't required for teenagers; therefore, Brutus probably didn't hate me or Black people. During the Morrison unit, I was a heavy hitter for the role of mothers in a family unit. In other words, the students were assigned to write an "ode to mothers"; class discussions centered on how mothers shape the health of the family; the assigned summer reading book was *The Color of Water: A Black Man's Tribute to*

His White Mother by James McBride; and students shared their personal thoughts and academic understandings of their mothers throughout the unit. Every class period, I unconsciously triggered trauma for Brutus.

Ego lives an unconscious life, shattering others. I continue to make mistakes. Forever changed by Brutus, however, I strive to live a more conscious life. I am ashamed of my blind pride; I pulled the race card on an innocent child. I never accused Brutus face-to-face of being a racist, but my egotistical mind almost destroyed a lifeline to the future. In my last class for the year with Brutus, I publicly apologized to him for not being compassionate and seeking first to understand him before being understood. He gave me the most beautiful smile and said, "It's okay, Dr. Hobbs. We all make mistakes." I proceeded to tell him that I had undergone some cancer testing and remarked on how life shapes us into stronger and more resilient people. Brutus asked if my tests were positive, and I revealed that they were negative. He then said, "I am so glad that you are okay." I thanked him and said, "I love you, and I am so sorry that life has been so hard for you." He said, "I love you too." There wasn't a dry eye in the entire classroom that day. Another lotus flower had just been added to my memory garden. His beauty is forever in my heart. The lotus flower can endure any extreme climate. Flooding may tear a lotus's entire root system, but the seeds always survive. The seeds can survive thousands of years without water. The flowers grow out of mud, and they purify the water in their opaque environment. Every night, they submerge themselves into the murky and muddy water; every morning, they bloom again without any residue.

Teachers rarely have opportunities to discuss the sanctuary feature of the profession. We are too exhausted, battered, or invisible for the world to notice. But our students notice us, care about us, and love us, I think. Despite the heaviness of their backpacks, they manage to enter our classrooms trusting complete strangers, at least initially, to lead the way. Quite often, we provide shelter from heavy storms; we apply salve on open wounds; we push them through the gates to freedom; we restore broken dreams; we paint brighter days ahead; we widen their scope of understanding; we serve as extended family. Sometimes, families collide.

After we had finished the unit on *The Bluest Eye*, one of my students who is Asian approached me after school with a wrapped gift in her hands. I will call this student Celine. Much to my surprise, Celine told me that she had purchased this gift with her own money, and she wanted me to have it. We are not supposed to accept gifts, but this gift was an expression of Celine's heart, and I didn't want to disrespect her good intentions. As I unwrapped the gift, she told me that she wanted me to have this replica of a Korean doll dressed in traditional apparel because it symbolized her identity and her desire to celebrate and extol her culture. I was deeply moved until she began to cry and doubled over in sadness. I took her hands and asked her to sit down, after which I gathered a tissue packet from my purse and gave it to her. She proceeded to tell me that Morrison's book had really changed her life. She intimately understood the pressure to conform to an ideal beauty image; she understood wanting to be accepted so badly that poor decisions made to achieve perfect beauty could result, with tragic consequences. I listened intently, still unsure of what her impassioned connection to the pressures of an ideal beauty image was.

As she gathered her composure and began to explain her emotional reaction, I found myself in awe of a young woman who had decided to openly defy her family. I hadn't known that my instructional lessons might challenge her cultural upbringing. Celine taught me that it was common practice for an Asian female to get cosmetic surgery on the eyes. Celine shared with me that her family had purchased a plane ticket for her to return to South Korea to get the procedure. She understood that this would be her high school graduation gift. Admittedly, she was still unsure about her decision because her family was placing a severe amount of pressure on her to get the procedure. Although her mind was unclear, her heart was rooted in loving the eyes staring back at her from the mirror. I admired her heart.

Despite my sometimes wavering self-esteem, I try to serve as a positive influence regarding self-love to all of my kids. I tell them that they are perfect just as they are and to love every part of themselves. I'd had no idea that Asian females suffered from the same pressures to conform to White standards of beauty. Celine and I talked for at least an hour after school about our shared vulnerabilities and varying degrees of Lucifer moments. We cried; we swapped stories; we hugged. We entered a lonely sacred space together and discovered that we each had a friend. I still have my beautiful Korean doll; the red attire is still as vibrant as the day I received it. Every now and then, I glance over at the eyes: flawless, immaculate, and untouched. I smile.

The Ancient One says to Marvel's Dr. Strange, "Silence your ego, and your power will rise." Quite often, truth in fiction is guidance from the divine realm. The divine realm gives earthly beings access to otherworldly understandings in the form of creativity. When we observe, listen, and seek to understand the unknown and receive clarity, we are being instructed, guided, and inspired by the spiritual world. Spirit guides and angels surround us in love during every moment, every second, every hour of our existence. If you are still, silent, and full of positive thoughts, words, and actions, you will hear them, and you might be granted the sacred privilege of actually seeing them and feeling them hold you. They crave a connection with us just as much as we crave a connection with them. Intuition, that sixth sense, that extra "Spidey sense" mentioned by Spiderman, that third eye chakra perception, that hunch, that gut feeling, that instinctual awareness—these are the various ways in which our spirit guides and angels try to reach us. Our mind noise and nonstop lifestyle distort the message, and we may react or interpret our intuition incorrectly. Our divine Creator has provided all kinds of wonderful gifts to guide our earthly journey so that we may grow our souls. Animals and Mother Nature are among those many gifts. Comfort, peace, security, and understanding are easily accessible to all who hunger and thirst for it. "Come unto me, all ye that labor and are heavy laden, and I will give you rest" (Matthew 11:28 KJV).

If you want tranquility, if you want to be at peace with what is, and if you want to unlock the divine gifts, you must meditate. Meditation has many forms; I encourage you to find the form that suits you. Love and stillness allow me to hear God. Many spiritual leaders proclaim that our prayers allow us to talk with God. Meditation requires that we listen for our answers from the Divine One.

CHAPTER 7

Love and Stillness

*If I could speak all the languages of earth
and of angels, but didn't love others, I would
only be a noisy gong or a clanging cymbal.*
—1 Corinthians 13:1 (NLT)

ALL OF US want it. All of us need it. But do we really understand the meaning of love? I thought that I did until I began reading books about near-death experience, or NDE. The most important learned lesson: ego does not live in love. Life is quite amusing to me now as I ponder my roller-coaster ride with my own self-esteem. Because of my lack of self-love, I presumed my ego was quite low. Upon gaining a much clearer view of ego, I woefully realized that my ego is totally out of control. I love to win an argument; I love to bask in my academic achievements; I love attention; I want acknowledgment and appreciation for my hard work; I feel more comfortable controlling situations; I feel safe in an ordered, predictable universe; I busy myself with check-off lists so that I feel a sense of accomplishment; I don't want to be still because I have things that need to get done; I want to be loved or at least well-liked; I want to feel important; I want to matter; I don't want to be vulnerable; I want many things quickly; I want power, privilege, and status. I, I, I. I am not humble.

I know what some of you may be thinking: what's wrong with wanting to be loved or to matter? Nothing is wrong with these desires except for one major flaw in thinking. I am already loved, and I have always mattered. You are already loved, and you have always mattered. However, we don't always feel love, do we? I know that some people don't even believe true love exists. Let me share a story and technique with you.

Many years ago, I had reached an extremely low point in my life. I was driving along East River Drive, renamed Kelly Drive, in honor of Grace Kelly's brother John. My life had taken a miserable turn; I was crying uncontrollably and licking some bitter wounds of unhappiness. I felt utterly confused, alone, and most of all unloved. As I drove the road twisting and turning around the Schuylkill River, I replayed all of my mistakes in life, and my heartache seemed quite unbearable. "Share My World" sung by Kem came on the WDAS radio station, and I lost emotional control, though luckily not the control of the car. I found a small area along the drive to park the car and listen to the lyrics while my shoulders and chest heaved in pain and the tears from my childhood, adolescence, and adulthood flooded my eyes. The lyrics combined with the musical notes and soft, sultry voice of Kem released me; the song sanctioned catharsis.

In 2020, my evolving spirit embraced this song as a personal anthem of hope and love. In reality, most people would say that Kem is obviously singing to his love interest with the opening lines of "if it makes any difference, I still love you, girl." And this may be, in fact, true. Nonetheless, I imagine that God is singing the song to me. When I change the characters to God and myself, my life surrenders to the will of the Universe, and I am cloaked physically, mentally, emotionally, and spiritually—totally—in love. The experience propels me into sheer ecstasy. Ecstasy is a spiritual encounter; it's neither a sexual nor a narcotic experience. Unfortunately, when the word "ecstasy" is used, folks assume sex and/or drugs are involved. For me, the magnitude of the song's message gives me an overwhelming feeling of joy, happiness, and spiritual euphoria. I feel God's love for me; it moves through me, around me, out of me. This experience is also called transcendence. I am in the seat of perfect love. As I evolve, I am learning not to confuse sensuality with sexuality. Transcendence is sensual, not sexual. As I evolve, I am learning not to confuse love with lust. Transcendence is pure love. I have also learned that I have searched for pure, perfect love from another earthly soul who is also evolving. Rumi said, "Love is the house of God and you are living in that house." Shakespeare wrote extensively about the "ecstasy of love."[25] We search desperately to have a love that transcends time, space, and place; we search desperately for the perfect love that captures our mental, emotional, physical, psychological, and spiritual dimensions. We seek that which we already have. Isn't life marvelous? Now, some human beings connect with a partner on every level; when they make love, it is sensual, euphoric, spiritual, and transcendent. This type of coupling is a divine one; perhaps they are soul mates to one another. When they were choosing their souls' mission, they chose to connect again in the earthly realm. These are just reflections and meditations of my heart. Perhaps they may resonate with you.

I will pose a question. What do you think the biblical Song of Solomon is about? It is quite sensual, passionate, and powerful. Did you know that some scholars suggest that this particular book in the Bible is a love song from God to the Israelites? Maybe "Share My World" could be my love song from God. Maybe you have a love song from God as well. Have you ever listened to a song and found that its message, theme, melody, or harmony just brings you sheer joy or happiness or laughter? Is there a song that takes you to another place or plane and fills your heart with the "ecstasy of love," and while you listen, everything is right in the world, and you escape the war of the worlds? If so, this could be your love song from the divine realm.

Zora Neale Hurston via Janie in *Their Eyes Were Watching God* said, "Two things everybody's got tuh do fuh theyselves. They got tuh go tuh God, and they got tuh find out about livin' fuh theyselves."[26] My method is my manner of living for myself. When my journey presents seemingly insurmountable challenges that try to sabotage my self-worth, I go to God for myself and acquiesce to his perfect benevolence. Try it. Find a song about perfect love and then change the characters, close your eyes, be still, play the song, and let your heart soar. I hope it works for you. During the pandemic, I have found myself listening to my special anthem quite frequently. The divine realm, if you open yourself, has creative, sometimes comical ways of contacting us, supporting us, protecting us, and showing love toward us.

Regardless of my earthly placement, position, rank, or reputation, I have always mattered to and been loved by God/Source/the Divine One/Universe. Traditionally, I have cast my gaze outward, seeking to acquire a divinely bestowed gift from another earthly form. However, prior to my earthly arrival, I was already embraced in perfect love.

I affirm what many other authors, mystics, psychics, and evolutionary spiritualists such as Wayne Dyer, James Redfield, Doreen Virtue, Eckhart Tolle, Don Miguel, Paulo Coelho, James Van Praagh, Michael Singer, and Esther and Jerry Hicks proclaim: we began our earthly journeys as spiritual beings. Spiritualists assert that we are spiritual beings who desired an earthly existence. We existed in heaven with God, and we wanted to develop and expand our souls by choosing to have an earthly life. We chose our bodies/walks in life; we chose our parents; and we chose how we wanted to live and how we wanted to die. We have been given spiritual guides and guardian angels to assist us. What we think, say, and do affects a tidal wave of events because we are all interconnected. Every thought, every word, and every act emits a type of energy. So if I think, speak, and act positively, positive energy is released into the world/universe. If I think, speak, and act negatively, negative energy is released into the world/universe. COVID-19 is not a surprise to me, nor will any other world pandemic surprise me; if there is enough negative energy expelled into the universe, we are going to suffer from biological viruses and diseases and emotional and psychological plagues like hatred. And Mother Nature/Earth simply follows our lead. Think about these words: "And God said, Let us make man in our image, after our likeness: and let them have dominion over the fish of the sea, and over the fowl of the air, and over the cattle, and over all the earth, and over every creeping thing that creepeth upon the earth" (Genesis 1:26 KJV). It's simply the Law of Attraction at work.

I really don't believe that God is angry with us and punishing us; I think we are punishing ourselves. God has suffered defamation of character; God has been slandered, misrepresented, and vilified. I fully admit that life brings some twists and turns that my earthly self doesn't understand. However, when I become still and silent and/or read quietly, answers begin to unfold for me. In stillness, I access my spiritual side. I often visit parks with water nearby; gazing into trickling water provides a small escape hatch from the world at war. In these moments, I sometimes ponder: Why are my people suffering so much? Have our ways of thinking and acting brought our turmoil? Is it ever possible to have world peace? Why do babies and children have to die? Because we, generally speaking, like linear movements and causal explanations in life, my questions are suited to a linear and causal way of thinking. My questions lack spiritual depth; these questions are reflections of my earthly self, which forgets its divine connection sometimes. So I decide to reframe the questions using a more spiritual perspective: How is the suffering of my people awakening the world to injustice and the inhumanity bestowed upon others? Given the endured suffering of my community, why aren't we so proud of our achievements that self-hatred could never be an option for any of us? Would world peace bring self-righteousness and draw humanity further away from God? Does the death of babies and children shock families into becoming more loving by showing them how precious life really is? I am beginning to consider that the tragic demise of a totally innocent person is a message for those who survive rather than an utter destruction of the life taken. I keep recalling that we chose our walks and deaths in life. There is a divine plan in place; events occur for a reason. When the initial shock of a personal traumatic event passes, and the emotional pain subsides, I ask myself, *Okay, what am I supposed to be learning, understanding, thinking, or doing as a result of this situation? How is my soul or spiritual self growing?*

One day when my mother was nine months pregnant with my sister, Jocelyn Deidre, I was picked up early from school by my maternal grandmother (Mommom). I assumed that I would be cuddling my sister soon and couldn't wait to see and smell her. I have always loved the smell of babies. Years later, even after my daughter had reached the age of eight years old and refused to use it anymore, I would continue purchasing the Johnson & Johnson baby wash just to get a whiff, so that I could relive the experience of her being placed in my arms after her first bath in the hospital. I loved to run my nose through her very full and thick head of hair. Simply divine. Well, I didn't get a chance to hold my sister that day or any day at all. My mom had delivered a stillborn infant. She'd had a healthy pregnancy for the entire nine months. I remember being told that my mother went into labor, and my dad took her to the hospital, but the doctor refused to deliver Jocelyn because the contractions were too far apart; he sent my mother home. According to my mom, she knew when baby Jocelyn died; she said that she felt her life "fly out" (my mother's words) that evening. Painful and traumatic, absolutely. Nonsensical, perhaps, at the time. I recently learned that Jocelyn and my mommom are my spirit guides.

So what does all of this information have to do with love? And what is love? Because we are both divine and earthly beings, our lives intersect, and our earthly journey is supposed to assist our understanding of love, and we are supposed to help one another too. Everything we think, say, and do affects our understanding of love; if we disrespect another person, we are teaching the other person about how love works; if we encourage and support another person, we are teaching the other person how love works. If we hate another person, we are teaching the other person how love works; it works horribly, which translates into love not working at all. "For as he thinketh in his heart, so is he" (Proverbs 23:7 KJV). These earthly lessons will either stunt our soul's growth or allow our soul to flourish. If our soul does not flourish to the degree we "contracted" while in heaven, then we may have to return in another form until we successfully meet our goals. I don't know about you, but I would like to struggle now, dissolve my ego now, and learn as much as I can about love so that I may experience the rich wonders of my earthly existence. It would be inappropriate for me to condemn, challenge, disrupt, or attempt to repair anyone's definition or image of love. For me, however, love lives gracefully, expecting nothing in return. For me, love does not exist in a "quid pro quo" relationship. God doesn't love me because of what garments I wear or don't wear. God doesn't love me because of what I think or don't think; God doesn't love me because of what I say or don't say; God doesn't love me because of what I do or don't do. God loves me simply because *I am*. This is the very essence of love. Love is life itself: majestic and always divinely designed!

I believe parental love is supposed to resemble divine love at the earthly level. I presume that you love your child not because of the garments worn or not worn; you love your child not because of what they think or don't think; you love your child not because of what they say or don't say; you love your child not because of what they do or don't do. Unconditional love means loving unconditionally. You love your child because *they are*! This mirrors the beauty of our relationship with God, our divine Creator. We need to move into loving *what is.* For some of us, these thoughts on love move out of focus when love is seemingly unreciprocated or met with hostility or even violence. I am trying to learn how to love like God. I am trying to separate hateful T-shirts, gestures, thoughts, words, and actions from the beautiful souls who have disconnected from their spiritual essence because of sustained and unhealed trauma—because no matter what I think, say, or do, I know that I am loved unconditionally by our divine Creator; *we*, all of us, are.

Since I was at least eight years old, I have been able to recite these scriptures:

- *But I say unto you which hear, Love your enemies, do good to them which hate you.* (Luke 6:27 KJV)
- *But I say unto you, Love your enemies, bless them that curse you, do good to them that hate.* (Matthew 5:44)
- *Bless them which persecute you: bless, and curse not.* (Romans 12:14 KJV)
- *And be ye kind one to another, tenderhearted, forgiving one another, even as God for Christ's sake hath forgiven you.* (Ephesians 4:32 KJV)
- *This is my commandment, That ye love one another, as I have loved you.* (John 15:12 KJV)

Neither recitation nor memorization, neither deliberation nor cogitation, will grant our world liberation from the horrors of racism. We are parents to every child, and we are children to every parent. We must take what we know and do the work!

I will close this chapter with a short story. Soon after my daughter learned to speak using more complex sentence structures, she said to me, "Mommy, I chose you." I responded, "Huh, honey? What did you say?" She repeated, "I chose you." I had heard her the first time; I had just wanted to see if she would repeat it. I guess she determined from my facial expression that she needed to elaborate a bit more. She went on to say, "Mommy, when I was in heaven with God, I chose you to be my mommy. I saw you, and I told God, I want her to be my mommy." I thought her ideas were so precious, and I asked her if she would say that again. In fact, for about two years, she never deviated from the details of this wonderful story, and I recorded her on cassette tape (I know—those were the good ole days) telling me this story. At the time, I wasn't quite sure if I believed her, but I never criticized her or conveyed any form of doubt, I don't think. I just listened as she joyously told this story repeatedly for two more years. Despite the cassette tape recording, she doesn't remember saying these words anymore. Rather than searching for empirical evidence, I am choosing to be still and allow love to freely flow in and out of me while my soul just keeps learning.

CHAPTER 8

A Moral Imperative for Schools

Education is the passport to the future, for tomorrow belongs to those who prepare for it today.
—Malcolm X

AMERICAN EDUCATION HAS a moral imperative to eradicate racism. Not every person in America has a home, food, water, and security. But America has compulsory education. If you are homeless and between the ages of five and eighteen, you are required to attend school; if you live below the poverty line, and you are between the ages of five and eighteen, you are expected to attend school; if you live in a district that receives limited financial support from the government, and you are between the ages of five and eighteen, you must attend school; if you live in a district with greater financial resources, and you are between the ages of five and eighteen, you are required to attend school. The American classroom is the melting pot; the American classroom is the salad bowl; the American classroom is the most important thread that binds all of us together—we have an experience that bonds us together forever. Some of us live in the shadows, some of us live on the outskirts of life, and some of us live basking in the glorious rays of the sun. Although our environments, ethnicities, races, religions, genders, political affiliations, socioeconomic statuses, family structures, and other varying walks of life make us distinctive and lead us to sometimes wave different banners declaring war on opposing forces, we have gone to school from the age of five years old to the age of eighteen years old in the United States of America. Indeed, *E Pluribus Unum* echoes our educational existence. Therefore, this is where the work must begin; this is where the work should have begun. Unfortunately, African Americans didn't begin the race alongside White Americans because American schools were segregated, then moved to being "separate but equal," and currently reside in a post–*Brown v. Board of Education of Topeka* world. But we are still in a *Plessy v. Ferguson* state of mind and reality.

The "eracism" that we seek cannot be achieved until we implode our school systems. Why? If we truly believe that "all men are created equal" and that no person is greater or lesser than another person, isn't it time we fully understand what that feels like? We all bear the burden of keeping a have-versus-have-not system in place. Maintaining our current structure of education does not align with our creed. In fact, our educational system never actually honored our moral stance at all. We currently have a system that allows some students to be "better" educated than others. Typically, the more money a district spends per student, the greater the education, right? Is there equality between a private school education and a public school education? Is there equality between a charter school and a public school education? Aren't you curious why some students consistently do poorly on standardized tests and why some students consistently excel on standardized tests? Do you want to know why "standardized" tests really exist? I mean, why they fundamentally exist and who is designing them? Most of our systems have been White-washed, especially our American schools. How can we eradicate racism if our educational system already supports it? The very vein that runs through all of our blood is a broken American educational framework. We need to rebuild the foundation and mission of school so that "school" and "education" become synonymous terms and concepts.

CHAPTER 9

A New School = Education + Medicine

SCHOOLS ARE PRISONS for young people, regardless of color or creed. The inmates are released by bells to travel from cell to cell and given free time in the yard. They must ask permission to use the bathroom facilities, and our lockdown drills, which purportedly serve as practice for an impending harsh reality, only demonstrate a lack of understanding of the enemy within. Has anyone noticed that school shootings have been perpetrated by members of the school community? So many of us pose the question of why these tragic circumstances occur and reoccur, but have we asked how? For instance, how did the shooting in Sandy Hook occur? "How" questions lead us into the life of the shooter and the school community. The biography of a killer should never be celebrated or emphasized in the midst of a tragedy. Quite honestly, unfolding the biographical details at the time of an execution is tardily acquiring knowledge. It is imperative that educators begin to wrestle with how a school community fosters delinquent and deviant behaviors. How do layered history and trauma factor into the creation of an individual's decision to dehumanize another person to the point of execution? Let me be quite clear: schools don't breed murderers, but schools don't outsmart them either, and they should.

How does this small rant relate to racism? So many of my students have gotten lost in an unforgiving system that fails to see them. How do I know? They tell me. When you keep open lines of communication and build trusting friendships with young people, they will give their honest opinions; they will tell you both what you want to hear and what you don't want to hear. I have treasured every moment with my students. Listen, not every moment has resulted in serenity, compliance, and authentic scholastic learning. Some tearful and unsettling moments have provided learning opportunities of another sort: life lessons. In these ego-deflating moments, my students have taught me how to become a better listener, a more sensible evaluator, and a more pragmatic thinker. My students have taught me how to be a better teacher, and ultimately, they have fostered my development as a human being.

Education should seize its power! Unlike any other profession, education builds, changes, and rebuilds lives. Education can place salve on open wounds; however, schools are not hospitals currently. Currently, schools provide a safe haven for isolated individuals searching for a sense of purpose, mission in life, and career. The guidance department needs empowerment; guidance counselors didn't choose their profession because they wanted to engage in paper pushing. The role of "guidance counselor" should not be equated with paper pushing. We need to name our goals, outcomes, and roles in education and fulfill the duties implied by the nomenclatures. Otherwise, we belie our mission, and society at large cannot comprehend the contradiction and move in accordance.

Discord between stakeholders confuses and bemuses young people. Their bemusement is costing them their lives. Education can open doors that traditionally have been closed to marginalized youth; mentorship programs allow young people to explore various fields of study and develop professional and personal relationships with significant and caring adults. Many young people have difficulty connecting with adults who understand them. Although the aforementioned idea is not an epiphany, educators need to facilitate meaningful partnerships for every student, either within the school setting or via preceptorship. Education can open new levels of understanding for young minds. Educators cannot control the values and beliefs present in a child's home environment; however, an education that examines and scrutinizes a topic or issue from multiple points of view will allow a young person to carefully weigh and deliberate academic and personal life decisions. Simulating real events in the safety of a classroom setting while discussing the outcomes from multiple angles enables young people to move away from bigotry, chauvinism, and hatred. Simulations provoke engagement from the heart and the mind. Biased textbooks, study materials, and other resources must be eliminated. If unbiased texts cannot be found, they must be written. Until such time, current texts need full disclosures and explanations from educators in which the bias is unpacked. When a text or resource is unpacked, the point of view is revealed, the rationale behind the point of view is revealed, the era for the rationale is revealed, and the members of society who benefited from the point of view and the position of privilege in which they sit become exposed, along with the revelation of who was marginalized or somehow devalued as a result.

Watch Ava DuVernay's 2016 documentary called *13th* if you would like an extraordinary example of how African Americans have been groomed for prison. History courses need total implosion. An African proverb says, "Until lions have their historians, tales of the hunt shall always glorify the hunter." Making a unit on slavery the only effort at teaching Black history compromises, derails, and limits the knowledge of all students but especially African American students. Additionally, what angles, lenses, and perspectives are used during a unit on slavery? Where are the lessons on Fred Hampton or the history of any HBCU or lessons on the construction of famous and important historical buildings, like the White House and the United States Capitol, built by enslaved Black people? Teaching perspectives that overemphasize servant–master relationships does not reflect a commitment to diverse learners or divergent thinking. How many history courses consider revisionist history? How many history courses explore Black inventors? As a special exercise, try to function on a daily basis without using any inventions by an African American; I surmise you would not be able to function at all. Living history breathes all around us. What about lessons on African Americans who have recharged humanity and ushered in new ways of thinking, like Ava DuVernay, Michelle Obama, Ryan Coogler, Ruth E. Carter, and Mae Jemison, who has paved the way for NASA astronaut Jeanette Epps to be the first Black woman to join the International Space Station crew, scheduled for flight in 2021. We aren't just capable of dribbling and running balls up a court and down a field; we are changing the world. Malcolm Gladwell creates podcasts on historical revisionism in which each episode begins with an inquiry about a person, event, or idea and proceeds to question the received wisdom about the subject. We need a greater emphasis on inquiry in all subject matters. As the vestiges of systemic racism fall, so should our infrastructures that have supported racist ideology.

The Tactic and Strategy

Education and medicine must join hands in a happy matrimony. Think about this idea for a moment. If all of us are survivors and victims of trauma, then how are schools going to assist the cognitive functioning of their students if we, as educators, are in need of traumatic healing *and* our students are in need of traumatic healing? If all of us are trauma victims and survivors, we need the medical professionals to join us. Think of the airplane emergency model. Before I can assist my child, I need to aid myself. We are in a world emergency. Racism is a deadly disease destroying our humanity! COVID-19 has served two important life-sustaining purposes: (1) validation of the critical role of medical professionals to the physical, psychological, and biological needs of humanity and (2) reflection and stillness to reassess our core values and beliefs. In the midst of carnage, lessons on life emerge, if we choose to heed them.

Schools have been transitioning into hospitals for quite some time.

As a teacher, I am finding that I am ill-equipped to handle the rapidly changing physical, psychological, and biological needs of my students. Almost daily, new trauma profiles emerge in the classroom. COVID-19 has awakened the world to the significance of educators as well. The education of humanity is at stake. As a teacher, I am prepared to meet the cognitive needs of every student. I can hone and sharpen critical thinking, writing, reading, speaking, and listening skills. I can inspire, shape, and model lessons on life. I can help to repair damaged self-esteem. I can assist with identity and gender formation or no formation. I can problem-solve issues and prepare students for a job, a career, volunteerism, or entrepreneurship. I can help them balance a checkbook, solve an equation, conduct a science lab, complete a geometric proof, speak another language, explain the factors leading up to World War II, draw a self-portrait, build endurance for exercise, find Burkina Faso on a world map, or understand our cosmos. But I really need medical professionals to assist me with my students who are suffering from alcoholic parents, years of physical and psychological abuse, rage, proclivity for violence, desire for self-harm, desire to hurt others, or any other physical, psychological, or biological trauma. Teachers can't do it all, anymore. We are exhausted, frustrated, and quite frankly depressed and dejected. However, despite our traumatic experiences, we have learned to care for the academic, personal, and social needs of our students. It is time for an implosion of American schooling. Racism is the wake-up call for this implosion; it is the knell ringing in the death of our humanity.

Healing Americans embrace wholeheartedly the dream of Martin Luther King that Black people and White people should join hands, set aside differences, and fulfill the American dream together as a unified nation, under God, for liberty and justice. But the Americans who are not healing—who are too broken by their traumatic experiences, who are so filled with self-hatred, who need love—don't believe in the dream because it never existed for them, or it was destroyed a long time ago. Perhaps the dream for the non-healing is some nightmare locked in their DNA or past life. Perhaps for the non-healing, the nightmare is their daily lives. My hope tells me that most Americans are healing Americans—Americans who have faced trauma but still have the will and heart to face new challenges; they still have the heart to wrestle and struggle and gamble with new ideas, new systems of thinking, and new lives. What about the unhealing Americans who have lost their hearts? A person cannot perceive what is unknown. I cannot expect the unhealing American's heart to be in accord with my healing heart because my heart may present an inconceivable possibility.

So those of us with the strength, courage, and wisdom must assist the fallen, unhealing Americans who have chosen to fight the dream. The unhealing and fallen Americans are the racists, bigots, chauvinists, and other groups demonstrating hatred. Embrace your brothers, wrap them in a cloak of love, and demonstrate that the dream exists, and we can all heal our wounds together and, ultimately, heal Mother Earth. Climate change, in part, reflects human desires. Therefore, choose to abandon dark imaginings so that we may usher in a new dawn. We are on another "warm threshold"[27] of justice. Let the fields of education and medicine join hands to fulfill the American dream. The Spirit eternally extends an invitation; the mind and body just need to answer. Restorative practices may help the mind and body answer the invitation. Because schools in America are so beleaguered with rules and dos and don'ts, discipline and basic forms of communication require a victim and servant–master relationship—there are those with and without power; there is right and wrong. Unfortunately, the structure of school does not permit exploration of how and why. Why is a student consistently breaking the rules? Why are the rules needed? How did a student learn hate? Why does a student hate? The answers to the aforementioned sample questions require extensive work, research, and compassion. Reactivity and reactionary resolutions do not heal and resolve the pain within all of us. Educators examine the roots, stems, and leaves of a flower. The flowers, our students, deserve a more compassionate educational system to assist with the psychosocial, sociocultural, and sociopolitical areas of their lives. Restorative practices—a proactive approach—involve a core belief founded in social justice. A coalition between education and medicine founded under the principle of reconciliation can propel healing. Then the dream can begin earnestly for all of us.

CHAPTER 10

A Moral Imperative to My People

The Night is beautiful,
So the faces of my people.

The stars are beautiful,
So the eyes of my people.

Beautiful, also, is the sun.
Beautiful, also, are the souls of my people.[28]

SOMETIMES I ASK myself why I care so much about what people think of me. Why do I care about what people say about me? Why do I need to compare myself to literally everything under the sun? Within my soul, I know that I am not a bitch, nigger, or nigga; I am not a gangster either. I am not even a queen. I am far better than a queen. I am a divine, spiritual being created out of love, from love, and in love by God. I try not to gaze intensely into the mirror to fix things anymore. The mirror is not a reflection of me at all; it is a reflection of the outer coil I chose. Spiritually speaking, I am not completely sure why I chose this particular journey because it has been so dehumanizing. However, I do know that I am not who I used to be, and I am not quite who I will become. I am satisfied with who I am. Do you remember the statement many of our elders used to say and sing: "It is well with my soul"? Wisdom is slow-moving, but eventually, hopefully, and prayerfully, it arrives for all of us.

If our nation moves to fulfill its promise to us that indeed "all men are created equal," we must be ready to receive our blessing. Self-hatred is no longer an option or a choice. We will never be able to perceive love until we first caress self-love. In other words, we may not recognize the efforts exerted on our behalf if we don't learn how self-love looks, smells, tastes, sounds, and feels. If we can put into practice what we learn about ourselves, our knowledge will serve to help others and enhance our soul's mission. I know, now, that I can no longer endure waiting on others to acknowledge my worth, to tell me that I matter, to tell me "I love you." Self-love always commands respect.

Do not allow hatred to consume your hearts; I know how an automatic reaction of utter disgust can overtake a mind. I too was taught the rhyme "sticks and stones may break my bones, but words will never hurt me." Well, we know that adage just isn't true for us! Words and actions have broken my spirit, my mind, and my body's self-image. Let me share a final story from my teaching career.

One particular year, I couldn't wait to inherit my new students for the Advanced Placement literature and composition course. Their reputation for brilliance, work ethic, and overall kindheartedness preceded them. My colleagues raved about these kids. So as their future twelfth-grade English teacher, I eagerly anticipated their arrival in my classroom.

Occasionally, I break from the academic rigor to engage in lighthearted, extended conversations with all of my classes. It is important, as a teacher, to bond with students; it builds trust and compassion. I am not sure how my dad's personal narrative got woven into the fabric of discussion on this day, but it did. My dad, born in 1934, grew up in a very small, dirt-road town named Butler in Georgia. One of our family vacations returned us to his birthplace, including his one-room schoolhouse, which was still standing after fifty years. My dad grew up on a farm, and he and my uncle Johnny had very little to eat because the Hobbs family of Butler, Georgia, were dirt poor. My aunt Beulah, also nicknamed Beauty because she epitomized the word, never lived on the farm with my dad because she was the offspring of my paternal grandfather's extramarital affair. My dad told me that he and Uncle Johnny used to hide in the barn whenever my grandparents fought because each of them owned a pistol, and when they had an argument, they would shoot at each other. Even though I never learned how many times they really argued in this manner, I do know that both of them were "terrible shots"—Grandma Hobbs and Grandpa Hobbs, as I called them, died in their late seventies and not from any gunshot wounds.

In spite of dire poverty and Grandpa Hobbs's frequent spells of drunken behavior and domestic violence, my dad took comfort in caring for his little pet piglet, who went everywhere with him. The piglet walked him to church, scampered along with him during chores, and slept with him in his bed. One morning, my father awakened to the squealing of his pig, only to discover my grandpa killing his pet pig with an axe. You see, my dad's family was so poor that the full-grown pig would now be food for the family of four for the next week. Grandma Hobbs salted the pig and preserved it for family dinners. My dad had no other choice but to eat his pet pig for an entire week.

Eventually, my dad's family migrated to the North and settled in West Philadelphia. Prior to graduating from Dobbins Technical High School, my dad, quite brilliant in the area of electrical engineering, had impressive job offers from companies such as Philco and RCA. My dad still has the first transistor radio that he built over fifty years ago. My dad's career led him to become a senior electrical engineer with Unisys and NASA. In fact, my dad led the engineering team that literally turned on the first mainframe computer in Japan, and he was a part of the engineering team that built the radio system for the Apollo 15. I remember visiting NASA as a child and sitting in the NASA lunar spaceflight excursion module. I also remember when my dad took a break from work and my parents and I went to the beach on the Gulf of Mexico. A White man approached my dad while we were lying on our towels and told my dad that we were on a segregated (Whites only) beach. My dad said, "I don't care!" I thought we were going to get in trouble and be asked to leave or worse—get arrested. Nobody else bothered us that day, but boy, did folks just stare at us. My dad's life brings me to my knees in honor of his resilience, strength, and courage. I am grateful for his love. Unfortunately, you won't find my dad's name on Wikipedia or any other privileged, abridged resource on people of historical significance. His ethnicity and race, along with his humble demeanor, didn't fetch him any societal praise or recognition.

This is the story I shared with my AP class composed entirely of White students. When I arrived to my AP class the next day, a brand-new packaged slab of Oscar Mayer bacon sat on my desk.

Something in me broke that day. I have spent years trying to heal that wound. I have hoped and prayed for relief; I have hoped and prayed that my hurt wouldn't reflect outward; I have hoped and prayed that my vulnerability would never be ravaged again. I have hoped and prayed for my heart to place the incident in my past and make it disappear. But every act or message of hatred and violence from White people against my people conjures painful memories, especially this one. Eventually, I settled into my feelings of discomfort and no longer look into the eyes of my students with a sense of self-hatred. This episode didn't move me outward; it moved me inward. My Lucifer moment became self-destructive. Going forward, I wasn't as forthcoming with my personal stories with my students, and I learned how to walk the line of contentment again by keeping my vulnerabilities private.

Years later, I received an email from a member of that AP class, asking for a recommendation for a high-clearance job with the United States government. I cheerfully wrote the recommendation, emphasizing all of my former student's magnificent academic and personal attributes, even though I knew this student was the one who had physically placed the bacon on my desk. I made the conscious decision to place my ego aside, drain the swamp of my misery, and love myself enough to forgive these former students.

I set myself free, and it felt glorious! A funny thing happened a couple of years later. I was in a local establishment, and the parent of one of my former AP students from that fateful year recognized me. We chatted for a bit, and then the parent told me that her child was so incredibly sorry for what had happened to me that year and how her child had wanted to apologize to me. The parent was so sincere and endearing. I thanked the parent and left the establishment. I absolutely loved her child and still do, and I always will.

Nothing happens by chance; our lives unfold in majestical ways. The love I expected from others didn't occur until I loved myself. Loving *always* requires forgiveness. Remember, no person is greater or lesser than another, and all of us make mistakes. Forgiveness is such a lovely act—it frees your mind, it frees your body, and it frees your soul! Depending on the severity of your emotional, physical, and mental pain, forgiveness may not be easy. Swallowing that ego—ugh, it stings so badly to do it. When I know consciously that I need to dissolve my ego, my stomach hurts, and my mouth feels full of cotton balls, and occasionally, I feel too vulnerable. Despite the physicality, your soul's power gains momentum as a result. Ego suppression releases you to live your soul's mission. Some White people are unaware of what they don't know. Privilege grants a type of impervious skin coating or shield. When I am wrapped in a cloak of defeat, disillusionment, and doubt, I travel to my memory garden of lotus flowers. My lotus flowers transport me to a place of healing, light, and conscious living. When I think of the racist thoughts of others, I am reminded of my own erroneous and detrimental thoughts. I remember that we all make mistakes; I remember we are all the same despite apparent differences. I remember Brutus.

We must live the dream we desire. We must disrobe ourselves of the cloak of ugliness soaked in self-hatred and self-doubt. If we compromise our integrity with thoughts, words, and actions of colorism, how can the demand for equality be met earnestly and honestly? Let's not worsen the dehumanization and create unwarranted trauma within our own community. We should reconsider our method of disciplining our children as well. "Spare the rod, spoil a child" belongs to an older form of consciousness. Do you think beating our children into obedience and submission fosters or hinders self-esteem? Do you think we have absorbed and followed the master narrative far too long?

As an African American mother, daughter, woman, cousin, friend, schoolteacher, colleague, associate, and stranger in the streets, I know that folks are watching me. I am always wrestling with self-love, quite honestly. This relationship reflects outward and influences outwardly. As I struggle within, I meditate on the following verse: "Then said Jesus, Father, forgive them; for they know not what they do" (Luke 23:34 KJV). Once my mediation ends, I walk forward into the horizon; sometimes I might even skip.

CHAPTER 11

Healing

Give me love, love is what I need
to help me know my name.
—Seal, "Love's Divine"

THE MURDER OF George Floyd shocked me into an interior space of unbridled pain. Now I am choosing to be whole; I am choosing to absorb light; I am choosing to focus on life rather than death. I am choosing to forgive. However, if I allow the tragic events of the day to direct my thoughts, if I allow previous moments of suffering to direct my journey, if I use historical events to shape a belief system, if I close the door to my enemy, then I invite hatred to reside in my mind and heart. Once Lucifer takes my hand, the opportunity for healing moves farther away.

Every single human being has suffered some type of trauma; some folks have suffered much worse than I, and some folks have suffered less than I. We don't need to weigh, sort, categorize, and label our individual heartaches, thereby creating a competitive tournament of the fittest. The notion of survival of the fittest belongs to an outdated consciousness; it boldly asserts ego. How about using our collective traumas to launch a healing crusade? This crusade must have love as its ultimate purpose; this crusade fully acknowledges that we are spiritual beings who chose our earthly forms in an effort to cultivate our souls. Our intricate and diverse earthly forms epitomize beauty. The negative words and actions of human beings do not capture the essence of our humanity. Our true spirit seeks expression via kind words and gestures, compassionate hearts, contemplative conversations, polite honesty, hope, forgiveness, and conscious and selfless living.

For some people, the brutality of the trauma makes forgiveness seem impossible or perhaps not an option. Then let me ask a question: have you tried mercy? This is exactly what George Wallace, former governor of Alabama, received. I remember several Sunday evening fireside conversations with my parents and grandparents about Governor George Wallace. When I was a child, just the pronouncement of his name gave me a feeling of uneasiness. I learned that this man had been supported by the Ku Klux Klan, and in one of his inaugural speeches, he said, "Segregation now, segregation tomorrow, segregation forever." He was the type of man whose words and actions solidified horror for African Americans. You have seen the famous photographs of Governor Wallace's "Stand in the Schoolhouse Door," preventing two Black students, Vivian Malone and James Hood, from enrolling at the University of Alabama. As a child, when I heard that the National Guard had needed to intervene, I understood that my country had hated me the moment I was born in 1966. Given Governor Wallace's stance in the 1960s and '70s, I really didn't comprehend why my parents groomed me for college. I just knew that if the National Guard needed to escort me there, I wasn't going. So racist ideology lived in the recesses of my mind from a very early age. I loved Reverend Dr. Martin Luther King, and if he said Governor Wallace was "the most dangerous racist in America," I believed him. So I garnered a good amount of fear in my life: fear that my skin, my hair, and my body would define my interactions with the world, and these interactions probably wouldn't go well. Some of the same hand gestures used by the former KKK-supported governor, I see being used today. Even though my daughter and I have finished our college educations, the Sunday evening fireside conversations, with just my dad now, still resonate with fear.

More recently, I started doing some research on Governor Wallace so that I could identify how and why this man received 90 percent of the Black vote when he ran for a fourth term in 1982. I discovered a fascinating article by columnist Jonathan Capehart of the *Washington Post*. In an interview, Capehart spoke with Representative Barbara Lee from California, who powerfully articulated her intergenerational history with politics and layered history with the "humiliation and segregation" of Jim Crow. Representative Lee not only organized the northern campaign for Shirley Chisholm, the first African American woman in Congress and "the first of her race and gender to run" for president of the United States, but also went to Miami as a delegate. The interview goes on to further highlight how Shirley Chisholm went to visit Governor Wallace in the hospital, after he had been shot and confined to a wheelchair for the rest of his life. Representative Lee recalled thinking, *How in the world could this woman* [Shirley Chisholm], *this Black woman, go visit this horrible individual?* Peggy Wallace Kennedy, daughter to the former governor and present in the interview as well, revealed that her father asked Chisholm, "What are your people going to say about your coming here?" According to Wallace Kennedy, Chisolm replied, "I know what they're going to say, but I wouldn't want what happened to you to happen to anyone." Wallace Kennedy went on to say that her dad was "overwhelmed by [Chisolm's] truth, and her willingness to face potential negative consequences of her political career because of him—something he had never done for anyone else." Representative Lee further stated that when she addressed "Miss C" (a term of affection for Shirley Chisholm), seeking to understand why she would ever visit a segregationist and a man who also was running for US president as an opponent, Chisholm said, "But sometimes we have to remember we're all human beings, and I may be able to teach him something, to help him regain his humanity, to maybe make him open his eyes to make him see something that he has not seen ... you know you always have to be optimistic that people can change, and that you can change and that one act of kindness may make the difference in the world" (*Washington Post*, 2019).

As human beings, all of us have the potential to become racist thinkers; we have the potential to speak words of hatred; we have the potential to execute violence. Hatred emanates from a spectrum of infinite shades and colors.

As human beings, all of us have the unbridled power to love others with our thoughts, words, and deeds. Love, too, emanates from a spectrum of infinite shades and colors. Unfortunately, we surrender the word too easily today. "Love you" misses the mark. When the "I" goes missing from the uttered sentence, the subject lives in the shadows, perhaps unsure of its own majestical existence and purpose. When we are born, we depart from a place of divine and perfect love and enter an imperfect earthly place in our self-selected bodies. Why? To find our way back to the divine love we've always known. T. S. Eliot said, "The end of all our exploring will be to arrive where we started and know the place for the first time." We chose our houses carefully and strategically because our selection directly impacts the journey of our soul. Some of us are more lost than others; some of us need assistance remembering that love. Regardless, all of us are infinitely and spiritually connected. When a fellow soul expresses hatred, look directly into the eyes of the soul and send love and light. Reframe an earthly confrontation; gaze into the eyes of hatred and remind the soul filled with hatred that it has gone too far from its truth. The only way you can bring a soul filled with hatred back from anger, despair, and its soulless journey is through example. "But I say unto you, That ye resist not evil: but whosoever shall smite thee on thy right cheek, turn to him the other also" (Matthew 5:39 KJV). This is a powerful instruction but an unnatural earthly response because of the level of emotional humility required. A natural, earthly response to confrontation, conflict, and any form of hatred is to return the exact response. But "an eye for an eye" (Matthew 5:38 KJV) is not the way!

More recently, I have tried to remember that the heart must be healed first before the mind can contemplate the right action. I try to remember that the relationship between the spirit, mind, and body is a deeply profound one that needs nurturing and healing constantly. As soon as I disconnect from the source of light, God, the universe, I jeopardize my relationship with myself and others; the mind-body-spirit alignment collapses. This disconnection from Source awakens pride, ego, and other negative energies. Thoughts, words, and deeds mobilize to meet the demands of the negative energy. When we are connected to our divine Source, we live with humility and compassion. Thoughts, words, and deeds mobilize to meet the demands of positive energies. I try to "humble [myself] in the sight of the Lord, and [know that] he shall lift [me] up" (James 4:10 KJV). I try to allow divine love to enter my heart so that it may radiate outward to others. I never understood that love could be so complicated and simple. I guess this may be why the earthly journey proves so challenging. Strengthening my soul so that it may return to the source of divine love with a transcendent understanding is not easy. But I know that I am not alone; I have 7.8 billion companions. Even if some of my companions choose to use their God-given possibilities to unleash a firehose on me, beat me, murder me, torment me, defile me, rape me, lynch me, burn me, desecrate me, or dehumanize me in any way, I will keep the door of healing open eternally.

I will try to remember that we are spiritual beings having an earthly journey; no person is greater or lesser than another person. I do remember that divine love binds all of us to God and that God loves all of us: the rich, the poor, the orphan, the child with parents, the victim, the criminal, the compassionate, and the racist. I try to remember to be still so I can receive my messages of hope, inspiration, and comfort from the angels and spirit guides. In reality, if the entire world was inhabited by only you, you would never be alone. If you cannot see and feel the divine realm, you may have disconnected yourself from Source.

I cannot force a single person into loving me; I cannot make a heart feel something that it refuses to know. However, I do believe the following:

Together, we can achieve heaven on earth. Jesus, a master teacher, said, "Verily I say unto you, except ye be converted, and become as little children, ye shall not enter into the kingdom of heaven" (Matthew 18:3 KJV). I am beginning to understand so many biblical scriptures for the first time. As an adult, I have always recognized children's beautiful qualities of innocence, nonjudgmental concern, care for others, speedy recovery from playground aches and pains, natural curiosity to explore the unknown, and sense of wonder. The fundamental childhood quality that often remains hidden is a child's ability to love without fully understanding the consequences of not loving. Love, in the world of adults, must be earned, respected, afforded, achieved, and granted. In the world of a child, love and forgiveness unite in friendship, oblivious to earthly toils. If we bravely and boldly face our traumas collectively, we can heal ourselves. Then our true spiritual selves and our innocence will be rediscovered; paradise will be found in the here and now.

Special Acknowledgments

All of my students who pushed me to the edge of the cliff and invited me to soar
Beth Hampton for her loving friendship in all seasons
My chosen family Chris and Dwight Martin
The Bloodlines: Cathey, Staley, Warner, Hobbs
Murrt for immortalizing my journey artistically
Laurie Doctor, who brought a healing light to a sacred space
The Warrior Women Artists of Quintessence, affectionately called my "Fifth Elements"
Kellee White for enlightening my soul's mission
Sean Hughes and the entire LMSD community for helping me to stand and walk
Kia Caldwell Photography and Keith Burroughs Sr for illuminating my spirit
My soul sister MSB
Stephanie E., a magnificent editor
Joseph E. Maenner & Associates, LLC, for legal advice
The keepers of secrets, spirits, and divine inspirations
Divine spirits in earthly bodies
May all of you find exactly what your soul seeks and learn exactly what your soul needs.
I love you.

Notes

1 Eckhart Tolle, *A New Earth: Awakening to Your Life's Purpose* (Viking Press, 2005), 150.

2 Tolle, *A New Earth*, 152.

3 Tolle, *A New Earth*, 152.

4 Zora Neale Hurston, *Their Eyes Were Watching God* (New York: Harper and Row, 1937), 14.

5 Toni Morrison, *The Bluest Eye* (New York: Penguin Books, 1970), 138.

6 Anita E. Woolfolk and Lorraine McCune-Nicolich, eds., *Educational Psychology for Teachers* (Englewood Cliffs, NJ: Prentice Hall, 1980), 51.

7 "Black Homicide Victimization in the United States," Violence Policy Center, accessed July 1, 2020, vpc.org.

8 Rachel Yehuda and Amy Lehrner, "Intergenerational Transmission of Trauma Effects: Putative Role of Epigenetic Mechanisms," *World Psychiatry* 17, no. 3 (October 2018): 243–57.

9 Tolle, *A New Earth*, 158.

10 Rachel Yehuda and Amy Lehrner, "Intergenerational Transmission of Trauma Effects: Putative Role of Epigenetic Mechanisms," *World Psychiatry* 17, no. 3 (October 2018): 243-57.

11 Tori DeAngelis, "The Legacy of Trauma," *Monitor on Psychology* 50, no. 2 (February 2019).

12 Tori DeAngelis, "The Legacy of Trauma," *Monitor on Psychology* 50, no. 2 (February 2019).

13 Paul Laurence Dunbar, "We Wear the Mask," *The Poetry Foundation*, accessed June 6, 2020, https://www.poetryfoundation.org/poems/44203/we-wear-the-mask.

14 Tolle, *A New Earth*, 131.

15 Woolfolk and McCune-Nicolich, *Educational Psychology for Teachers*, 56.

16 Tolle, *A New Earth*, 102.

17 Tolle, *A New Earth*, 81.

18 "Frida Kahlo Biography," *Biography*, accessed July 25, 2020, https://www.biography.com/artist/frida-kahlo.

19 Baha'u'llah, *Illumine My Spirit*, trans. Shoghi Effendi (Wilmette, Illinois: Baha'i Publishing, 2003), 171.

[20] Ralph Ellison, *Invisible Man* (New York: Random House, 1995), 243.

[21] Countee Cullen, "Incident," Baltimore Literary Heritage Project, accessed July 20, 2020, http://baltimoreauthors.ubalt.edu/writers/counteecullen.htm.

[22] Ellison, *Invisible Man*, 581.

[23] "Amish School Shooting in Lancaster PA," *LancasterPA.com*, accessed August 2, 2020.

[24] Lisa Lim, "How on Earth Did Our Planet Get Its Name? Not from a Greek or Roman Deity, That's for Sure," *South China Morning Post*, April 12, 2019.

[25] William Shakespeare, *Hamlet* (New York: Pocket Books, 1992), 79.

[26] Hurston, *Their Eyes Were Watching God*, 183.

[27] Martin Luther King, "I Have a Dream," speech presented at the March on Washington for Jobs and Freedom, Washington, DC, August 28, 1968, *American Rhetoric*, http://www.americanrhetoric.com/speeches/mlkihave a dream.htm.

[28] Langston Hughes, "My People," *PoemHunter.com*, accessed August 10, 2020, https://www.poemhunter.com/poem/my-people.

Bibliography

"Amish School Shooting in Lancaster PA." *LancasterPA.com*. Accessed August 2, 2020.

Baha'u'llah. *Illumine My Spirit*. Translated by Shoghi Effendi. Baha'i Publishing, 2008.

"Black Homicide Victimization in the United States." Violence Policy Center. Accessed July 1, 2020. vpc.org.

Cullen, Countee. "Incident." Baltimore Literary Heritage Project. Accessed July 20, 2020. http://baltimoreauthors.ubalt.edu/writers/counteecullen.htm.

DeAngelis, Tori. "The Legacy of Trauma." *Monitor on Psychology* 50, no. 2 (February 2019): 36-47.

Dunbar, Paul Laurence. "We Wear the Mask." *The Poetry Foundation*. Accessed June 6, 2020. https://www.poetryfoundation.org/poems/44203/we-wear-the-mask.

Ellison, Ralph. *Invisible Man*. New York: Random House, 1995.

"Frida Kahlo Biography." *Biography*. Accessed July 25, 2020. https://www.biography.com/artist/frida-kahlo.

Hughes, Langston. "My People." *PoemHunter.com*. Accessed August 10, 2020. https://www.poemhunter.com/poem/my-people/.

Hurston, Zora N. *Their Eyes Were Watching God*. New York: Harper and Row, 1937.

Lim, Lisa. "How on Earth Did Our Planet Get Its Name? Not from a Greek or Roman Deity, That's for Sure." *South China Morning Post*, April 12, 2019.

King, Martin Luther, Jr. "I Have a Dream." Speech, Washington, DC, August 28, 1963. *American Rhetoric*, http://www.americanrhetoric.com/speeches/mlkihave a dream.htm.

Morrison, Toni. *The Bluest Eye*. New York: Penguin, 1970.

Shakespeare, William. *Hamlet*. New York: Pocket Books, 1992.

Tolle, Eckhart. *A New Earth: Awakening to Your Life's Purpose*. North America: Viking Press, 2005.

Woolfolk, Anita E., and Lorraine McCune-Nicolich, eds. *Educational Psychology for Teachers*. Englewood Cliffs, NJ: Prentice Hall, 1984.

Yehuda, Rachel, and Amy Lehrner. "Intergenerational Transmission of Trauma Effects: Putative Role of Epigenetic Mechanisms." *World Psychiatry* 17, no. 3 (October 2018): 243–57.

Pg 28 " fulfilling a duty without
a heart beat
Transpersonal effect

Pg 41
*Pg 44 a sinner just like everybody else
Pg 44 Conscious living involves being in
the present moment, which align
with our souls purpose

Pg 14 (she destabilized my essent
*Pg 47
✓ Pg 48
‡ 52
Pg 67 Celene

Bristol + Maxine
Celine

Made in the USA
Las Vegas, NV
23 December 2022